# ANCIENT
# RUINS
## OF THE SOUTHWEST

An Archaeological Guide

# ANCIENT RUINS
## OF THE SOUTHWEST

*text and photographs*

*by* DAVID GRANT NOBLE

NORTHLAND
PUBLISHING

*To Ruth Meria*

FRONT COVER: *Lowry Pueblo Ruins north of Cortez, Colorado,
and Wukoki Pueblo at Wupatki National Monument north of Flagstaff, Arizona.*
FRONTISPIECE: *Cliff Dwelling III, Cedar Mesa, Utah.*

www.northlandbooks.com

FIRST REVISED EDITION, 1991
SECOND REVISED EDITION, 2000

Noble, David Grant.
Ancient ruins of the Southwest : an archaeological guide / text and photographs by
David Grant Noble.
p.   cm.
Originally published, c1981.
Includes index.
ISBN 13: 978-0-87358-724-2
ISBN 10: 0-87358-724-3
(alk. paper)
1. Indians of North America–Southwest, New–Antiquities–Guidebooks.
2. Southwest, New–Antiquities–Guidebooks. I. Title.

E78.S7 .N63 2000
979'.01–dc21                                                             99-049995

# Contents

# Preface

Y ou would not think a guidebook to ruins would need much revising. But archaeology is a dynamic scientific discipline and interpretations about the past are in a constant state of evolution. Take Chacoan roads: a generation ago, researchers thought they were long routes, extending for many miles from Chaco Canyon to far-flung communities. Today, however, the prevailing view is that most roads—and scores more have been recorded since the 1970s—were short, closely associated with great houses, and probably used for local religious processions.

In this new edition, I also wanted to expand the book because so many sites have recently been opened and interpreted for the public. Blackwater Draw in eastern New Mexico, for example, where the first Clovis points were found, now is open. And since their recent restoration, the stunning pictographs at Buckhorn Wash in Utah's San Raphael Swell can be fully appreciated. Only in 1996, did excavations begin at Bluff Great House, and an interpretive trail has been developed for the public. Other new interesting sites include the Romero Ruin outside Tucson and Palatki and the V-Bar-V Ranch Petroglyphs, near Sedona, Arizona. There's nothing new about Alibates Flint Quarries or Hueco Tanks, but they are both way off the beaten track and it took me awhile to get them in the guidebook.

In this expanded edition, I decided to reach further north into Utah to include several sites of the Fremont culture. The Fremont are known for their rock art, especially the imposing anthropomorphic figures such as can be seen at Dry Fork Canyon near Vernal. And nobody goes to Dinosaur National Monument for its archaeology, but they should.

*White House Ruins in Canyon de Chelly National Monument*

The main reason I wrote this book is because I love to explore the Southwest's mesas and canyons, find ancient ruins and rock art, and ponder their meaning. The process has deepened my appreciation of where I live and of those who lived here before me. I hope the words and photographs that follow lead to similar enjoyment on the reader's part. In this pursuit, however, we all have a responsibility to do what we can to further the preservation of our land's fragile and vulnerable archaeological treasures. In this regard, I would draw your attention to the Afterword, where preservation issues are discussed.

Many people have helped me develop this book. First to be mentioned are the past and present generations of archaeologists and scholars whose endeavors have produced such a wealth of data and knowledge about Southwestern prehistory. In particular, however, I would like to thank Kristie Arrington, Todd W. Bostwick, Doug Bowman, Bruce A. Bradley, J. J. Brody, R. B. Brown, Catherine M. Cameron, Charles Cartwright, Jim Collerem, Larry Davis, Joanne Dickenson, Paul Fish, John W. Hohmann, Laura Holt, Nina L. Hubbard, Winston Hurst, David Ing, Doug Johnson, Anne Trinkle Jones, Richard W. Lang, Stephen H. Lekson, Anthony Lutonski, Alex Mares, Reed E. Martin, Ruth Meria, John Montgomery, Peter J. Pilles, Robert P. Powers, James M. Rancier, Polly and Curtis Schaafsma, Cherie Scheick, Diane F. Souder, William B. Tsosie, Jr., and Dick Whitman.

# Introduction

The American Southwest contains the richest and most accessible collection of archaeological ruins in North America. The arid climate of this vast expanse of mountains, mesas, deserts, and canyons provides an ideal environment for preserving centuries-old pueblos and cliff dwellings, fragile pictographs, and the most delicate of artifacts.

To our good fortune, a few farsighted individuals over the past century have recognized the extraordinary cultural heritage of the region and successfully campaigned to have many archaeological treasures set aside as public monuments. This tradition continues today through the work of various governmental agencies, private organizations such as The Archaeological Conservancy (505/266-1540), and through the efforts of many generous individuals.

The Southwest's archaeological preserves form a remarkable and extensive outdoor museum. Numerous as these public parks and monuments are, they represent but the gleaming tip of an iceberg under whose waterline lie innumerable sites. They are our prehistorical library from which scholars methodically add to our knowledge of America's past.

In an age such as our own, when the pace of external change often exceeds our ability to adapt, ancient ruins can have more than a purely scenic or romantic appeal. Ruins are time anchors, giving substance to an elusive past. They memorialize the successes and failures of our predecessors and remind us of the mortality of civilization.

Accustomed as most of us are to physical comfort and convenience, it is only natural to regard the people of prehistory as "primitives." Their technologies, to be sure, were simpler. And yet, when we put aside material inventories, we soon discover that we moderns share many elemental challenges and experiences with the ancients. When you visit the sites described in the following pages, look for cultural comparisons rather than contrasts. Allow ruins and petroglyphs to serve as vehicles for time travel. In this way, the past will come alive.

Were the Sinagua of the upper Little Colorado River any less awed by Sunset Crater's eruption in the eleventh century than we were by that of Mount St. Helens in the twentieth? How did the problems of Hohokam shell merchants compare with the challenges of today's international traders? Was the Mesa Verdeans' search for fuel wood in the 1200s less urgent than our own quests for energy?

To be aware of the continuing shared concerns of human beings and the repeating patterns of history deepens and enlarges our appreciation of archaeology. And then weathered ruins and petroglyphs become more than mere objects of historical curiosity. As for the towers of Hovenweep or the monuments of Chaco Canyon, they take on an aspect of discarded theatrical sets from an age-old drama whose cast has changed but whose theme may once again be replayed.

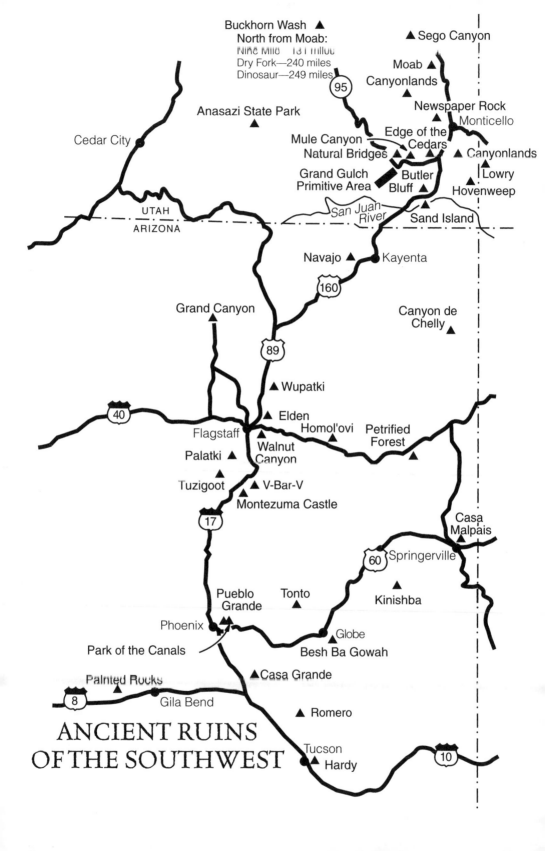

ANCIENT RUINS
OF THE SOUTHWEST

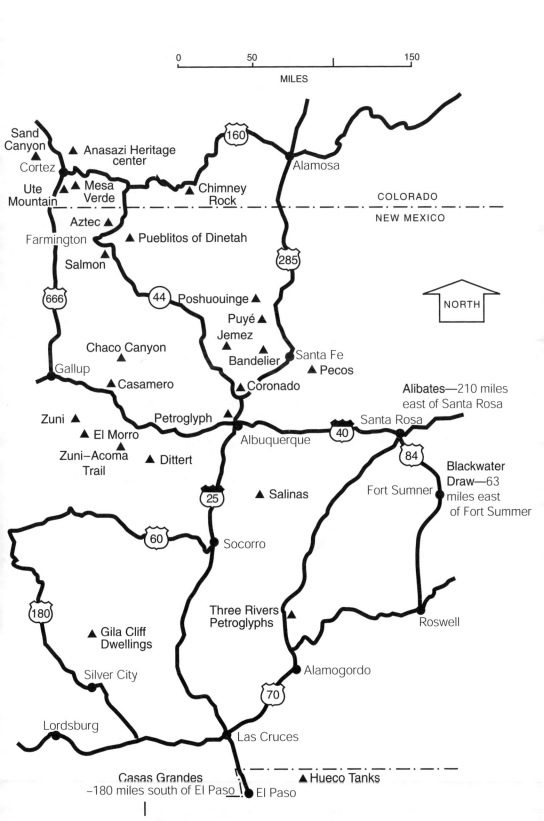

*George McJunkin, who discovered the Folsom Site.*
*Courtesy Museum of New Mexico, negative 50884.*

# The First Americans

U ntil quite recently, archaeologists had little notion how long human beings had been in North America or where Indians came from. In the nineteenth century, scholars speculated wildly about Native American origins—some even proposed that Indians once came here from Israel or Egypt.

The first solid evidence of the true antiquity of North American Indian culture came to light in 1925 on the Folsom Ranch in northeastern New Mexico. Here, some years earlier, ranch foreman George McJunkin, who had been born a slave, noticed some unusually large bones eroding out of a stream bank after a heavy downpour. McJunkin reported the find, and when archaeologists eventually excavated the site, they uncovered the bones of a long-extinct type of bison with spear points embedded among them. The Folsom Site established the presence of people in the Southwest about ten thousand years ago. Folsom Man, as he was dubbed, was a late Ice Age hunter-gatherer who roamed the lush savannas and woodlands of what are now arid plains.

Since the Folsom discovery, many more Paleo-Indian sites have been discovered from Canada to Argentina, and our knowledge of early America has grown. In the 1930s, Blackwater Draw (p. 7) near Clovis, New Mexico, produced distinctive fluted spearheads associated with mammoth kills that have been radiocarbon dated to over eleven thousand years old. They still represent the oldest evidence of human culture in the Southwest.

Archaeologists reconstruct a widely accepted scenario in which, toward the end of the last Ice Age, parties of hunters migrated from Siberia to Alaska over a land bridge that became exposed when ocean levels lowered. Traveling in small groups, they made their way southward along ice-free corridors, finding shelter in caves and rock shelters,

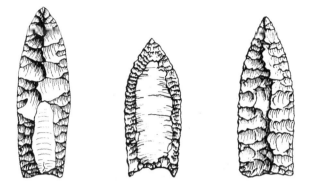

*From left to right: Clovis, Folsom, and Plainview points.*

probably fashioning tents or lean-tos from hides, and surviving off migrating herds of large animals or megafauna. Beyond a few stone or bone tools—most now deeply buried—these first Americans left scant evidence of their passing.

In 1997, confirmation that a site on the coast of Chile is 12,500 years old has suggested an even older chronology for the human experience in the Americas. People, it seems clear, had arrived in South America a millennium before they came to the Southwest. Today, scholars studying the evolution of New World languages are suggesting that the date of the first appearance of Native Americans in this continent may soon be pushed back even further. While Clovis remains indisputably the oldest known culture in the Southwest, the book is being rewritten about people who may have preceded them in other parts of the Americas.

It is important to note that archaeological theories regarding Paleo-Indian origins come from a distinctly Euro-American scientific perspective, which often is not shared by American Indians. Many traditional native people reject the notion of an ancestral migration from Asia. Instead, they adhere to their oral narratives, which recount how, in the beginning, their ancestors emerged from the earth into the present world, which has been their home ever since.

After the end of the Pleistocene epoch, the Southwest's climate became warmer and dryer. The big elephants disappeared, as did the Paleo-Indians who hunted them. After 5500 B.C., small bands of hunter-gatherers roamed the Southwest's varied environments in search of a subsistence. On their seasonal rounds, these seminomadic Archaic people gathered seeds, collected nuts, picked fruit, and dug roots and tubers to provide a nutritious diet, which they supplemented with protein from animals, birds, fish, and insects.

Eventually, knowledge of agriculture found its way to the Southwest and nomadism was largely replaced by a more settled way of life. This transition began around 1000 B.C. among the ancestral Mogollon (perhaps even earlier in southern Arizona) and eventually spread up to the Four Corners region.

It is important to remember that the time line of Southwestern pre-history is mostly taken up by hunter-gatherers. Some groups, like the Paiute, clung to their nomadic ways well into the nineteenth century, abandoning it only after it conflicted with economy and culture of white settlers and ranchers. Agriculture (not to mention industrial and post-industrial economies) was a relatively recent phenomenon. This fact is true not only of the Southwest, but throughout the world.

Suggested reading: *Search for the First Americans,* by David J. Meltzer, St Remy Press, Montreal and Smithsonian Books, Washington, D.C., 1993.

## Alibates Flint Quarries National Monument

*Alibates Flint Quarries National Monument is located near Fritch, Texas (northeast of Amarillo), in the Texas Panhandle. From Fritch, drive 6 miles south on Texas 136 and turn onto Alibates Road. Proceed 5 miles to the Bates Canyon information station. Guided walking tours leave here at 10 A.M. and 2 P.M. from Memorial Day to Labor Day, and off-season by appointment. (Call the monument to confirm schedule.) Information: (806) 857-3151.*

The making of tools from stone was the first technology developed by human beings, who discovered that certain types of stone, when broken in just the right way, took on a sharp edge that could be used to chop, scrape, or cut. Later, as the technology evolved, flint knappers learned to chip flakes off both sides of the stone, or core, to produce knives, spear points, and arrowheads.

Twelve thousand years ago, some of the Southwest's earliest human inhabitants found a series of rock outcrops along bluffs on the north side of the Canadian River that contained veins and nodules of chert (popularly called flint) of the highest quality for tool making. This flint occurs in a thick layer of dolomite, a Permian-age sedimentary rock resembling limestone. It was formed when mineral-bearing water seeped into the dolomite, replacing it with very hard, fine-grained quartz. Petrified wood is formed through a similar process. Like obsidian, the molecular structure of chert causes it to make conchoidal, or shell-like, flakes when fractured. It is this characteristic that allows knappers to make sharp-edged tools and weapons.

Besides its fine flaking qualities and hardness, Alibates flint had another characteristic that made it a popular tool-making material: its rainbow colors. This extraordinary stone comes in creamy whites, deep reds and brown, and translucent hues of gray, blue, and purple. A single flake can be banded in all colors; little wonder its appeal was so widespread.

An exposed chert boulder at Alibates Flint Quarries.

Archaeologists have found lance points made of Alibates flint at mammoth and bison kill sites dating from the Clovis and Folsom periods (see previous chapter). Archaic hunter-gatherers (6000 B.C. to A.D. 1) also prized this flint for tool making, as did their successors during the Woodland period (A.D. 1 to 1000). The quarries at Alibates, however, may have seen their most active use after the spread of farming, when the populations of the Southwest and surrounding regions burgeoned.

Archaeologists have investigated several Puebloan-style village sites in the vicinity of the quarries dating to between A.D. 1200 and 1450. (They have named this the "Panhandle Aspect of the Antelope Creek Focus of the Plains Village culture.") One of these sites, the Alibates Ruin, located less than a mile from the quarries, contained a substantial block of contiguous square, rectangular, and circular rooms of stone masonry construction. Its occupants farmed along the Canadian River and its tributary creeks and worked the quarries.

Demand for Alibates flint came from Indians who roamed the Great Plains as well as from agricultural people such as the Mogollon and Anasazi, who lived in the Rio Grande valley and beyond. The Alibates residents exported flint in exchange for a variety of items from far distant areas. Items excavated from Alibates area sites include, for example, obsidian and Pueblo pottery from the northern Rio Grande region of New Mexico, seashells from the Gulf of California and Gulf of Mexico, and pipestone from Minnesota. Clearly, the appeal of Alibates flint was the basis for widespread trade in the prehistoric period.

Archaeological excavations were first conducted at the Alibates Ruin in the 1920s, then again between 1938 and 1941, as a Works Progress Administration activity. In this early period of archaeological activity, research methods lacked sophistication and much data that might have helped later researchers interpret the site was not recovered. One wonders, for example, if the occupants of Alibates Village controlled access to the priceless quarries, and how they participated in the far-reaching trade network.

The Alibates quarries continued to be used well into the historic period. Nomadic Apache bands were present in the Panhandle region when Coronado searched the plains for the legendary Cities of Gold in 1541. In the eighteenth and nineteenth centuries, nomadic Indians such as the Comanches trailed the buffalo herds as they migrated across the Southern Plains. Until metal became readily available, these tribes, too, quarried Alibates flint to fashion their weapons.

At Alibates, do not expect to see large-scale excavations: the site's miners had only hand tools with which to dig their precious stone. They discovered that the buried chert was of higher quality than the weathered nodules found exposed on the surface of the ground. Archaeologists have recorded hundreds of pits covering approximately three hundred acres along a ridge top. The pits range from five to twen-

*Flakes of the colorful Alibates flint scattered on the ground.*

ty feet in diameter and are rimmed by mounds of lithic rubble, or tail-ings. Having been filled with windblown topsoil over the ages, they appear today as shallow depressions.

Quarry tours last approximately two hours. Your guide will lead you up a trail to the ridge and provide information on the geologic aspects of the site, flint-knapping methodology, and the prehistoric cultures of the Texas Panhandle region. Along the way, you will see chert nodules of various sizes and colors, many partially worked cores, and an abun-dance of colorful chips and flakes. All this debitage represents material that was rejected and left on the ground by ancient knappers. This is one type of litter to be grateful for!

Most people assume that the word Alibates is a Spanish term—Coronado explored this region in 1541—referring to the area where the quarries are located. In fact, an American cowboy settled here in pio-neering days: His name was Allen "Allie" Bates.

Suggested reading: *Lake Meredith National Recreation Area,* by Laurence Parent, Southwest Parks and Monuments Association, Tucson, Arizona, 1993. A wide selection of popular books on flint knapping is available, some of which are for sale at the mon-ument headquarters in Fritch.

# Blackwater Draw

*The Blackwater Draw Archaeological Site is located on New Mexico 467, 5 miles north of its intersection with U.S. 70. Information: (505) 356-5235. The museum is along U.S. 70, midway between Clovis and Portales, New Mexico. Information: (505) 562-2202. Entrance fee.*

Far out on the arid plains of eastern New Mexico, in a region known as the Llano Estacado, is the site, famous in archaeological circles, of Blackwater Draw. It was here, in the 1930s and later in the 1950s and 1960s, that archaeologists unearthed evidence of the Clovis Culture, the oldest in the Southwest.

Twelve thousand years ago, the Blackwater Draw site was a shallow, marshy, spring-fed pond surrounded by vast expanses of grasslands and limber pine forests. It was an ideal habitat for large grazing animals such as Columbian mammoths, cameloids, and horses, as well as their predators, including big cats, dire wolves, and people.

Over the millennia, human hunters waited among the bushes and reeds surrounding the pond for elephants, bison, and other game to come to drink. Imagine the ancient scene of a mammoth standing in the shallows or wallowing in the mud. Suddenly hunters rush out from their hiding places to thrust their spearshafts into the beast's vital organs. When it stumbles and falls, spearshafts snap off, their points buried deep within. After the animal's death, the hunters butcher it using long stone knives. Hunks of meat are carved from the huge carcass to be roasted and eaten on the spot or carried back to camp to be jerked for later consumption. The rest of the animal, mostly submerged in the water and mud, is left for scavengers.

Scenes like this were repeated over the generations and centuries. The bones and artifacts accumulated and were overlaid by deepening sediments on the pond floor. In time, the Clovis hunters were replaced by those of the Folsom Culture; then the Ice Age ends and Archaic hunter-gatherers camped nearby to hunt different game around the now dry pond. All the while, the pond's sediment layers deepened, sealing in the detritus to form a stratified record of the past. Eventually, the former pond became but a grassy depression in the seemingly endless reaches of New Mexico's buffalo plains.

The full realization of Blackwater Draw's potential as an archaeological site occurred in 1932 when the University of Pennsylvania commenced four years of excavations there. Of key significance was the finding of Clovis-period artifacts among bison bones that dated to between 11,040 to 11,630 years ago. Overlying this layer lay Folsom artifacts dating to 10,170 to 10,490 years ago.

*A mammoth kill by Paleo-Indians. Drawing by Richard W. Lang.*

Archaeological research at Blackwater Draw halted during World War II. But later, stimulated by a postwar road-building boom, digging of another sort took off here on a large scale: gravel quarrying. The next twenty years tell an amazing story of miners and archaeologists working in tandem; the first digging for stone, the second for bone. It is also a story of profit-driven private enterprise pitted against scientific research and cultural preservation. Since the gravel beds lay beneath the cultural layers, the overburden with its treasures of bones and tools had to be removed as quickly and efficiently as possible. By the late 1950s, heavy earth-moving equipment, combined with hydraulic suction pumps and blasting, was removing two hundred to four hundred cubic yards of sand, gravel, and overburden daily. Backdirt mounds were white with crushed bone and local artifact collectors were drawn to the feast.

The key find occurred in late 1962 with the uncovering of five mammoths and a bison along with many Clovis artifacts. Even the governor of New Mexico came out to see this archaeological treasure. One hundred thousand dollars was appropriated by the state legislature to acquire five acres of the site to be preserved in situ as a museum. But then, when the mining company demanded three times that amount,

*The excavations at Blackwater Draw show bones and artifacts from different time periods.*

7.000 B.P.  ARCHAIC PERIOD.

FOLSOM - MIDLAND

TEETH

JAW BONES

*Exhibit at the Blackwater Draw Museum.*

preservation efforts collapsed. The archaeologists could only encase their finds in plaster jackets for removal. Then the site was bulldozed.

In 1979, the 157-acre Blackwater Draw Site was purchased by Eastern New Mexico University. Thankfully, a small portion of the site, near the original pond's outlet, remains undisturbed. This area is being used for research and to train archaeology students. A modern shed covers one active excavation area where you can view layers of artifacts and bones from the Clovis, Folsom, and Archaic periods. Nearby, a small shed covers a hand-dug Clovis-era well. You can follow a rough interpretive trail around Blackwater Draw to learn about its archaeological and mining history.

There is more information about Blackwater Draw at the Blackwater Draw Museum located along U.S. 70 north of Portales. This modern museum building includes displays of spearheads and other artifacts, reconstructions of archaeological and geological deposits, interpretive dioramas, and publications for sale. A highlight for kids is a full-scale model of a mammoth's head complete with long upcurved tusks.

There are many travel services in Clovis and Portales.

Suggested reading: *The History of Blackwater Draw,* by Lienke Katz, Eastern New Mexico University, Portales, New Mexico, undated.

# Buckhorn Wash Pictograph Panel

*The Buckhorn Wash Pictograph Panel is located between Price and Green River, Utah, 22.5 miles east of Castle Dale. From the town of Green River, drive 30 miles west on Interstate 70 and take Exit 129; then continue 27 miles north on a well-maintained gravel road to the panel. From Price, take Utah 10 south for 29 miles, then watch for a sign and turn east. Continue 22 miles to panel. Information: (435) 381-5252 or (435) 636-3600.*

Not many years ago, the Buckhorn Wash Pictograph Panel was a notorious example of archaeological vandalism. For years, passersby had defaced the site with bullet holes, spray paint, chalk, and even axle grease from wagons. Happily, as part of the 1996 Utah Centennial Celebration, local preservationists arranged to have the panel restored. As a result, we are now able to appreciate the stunning beauty of these extraordinary prehistoric rock paintings.

While rock art is inherently hard to date, researchers are able to assign rough time periods to many sites. The Buckhorn Wash pictographs are estimated to be fifteen hundred to three thousand years old and exemplify the Barrier Canyon rock art style found in eastern Utah and in Canyonlands National Park (p. 76)—as well as in other nearby parts of the Colorado Plateau.

The creators of the paintings were Archaic-period hunter-gatherers who roamed over a wide territory and lived by foraging, hunting, and fishing. Although they traveled in small bands during most of the year, it is believed they would periodically gather at certain sites to enjoy social interaction and join in religious ceremonies. Such gatherings may have provided the context for doing rock art. Similarities between Barrier Canyon–style pictographs and later Fremont rock art suggest that the Fremont people may have been the descendents of the hunter-gatherers who made this and other panels in the region.

The Buckhorn Wash panel, which is more than a hundred feet long, includes groups of life-size anthropomorphic figures that have a supernatural or ceremonial aspect. Their strangely elongated bodies seem to hang eternally suspended in lithic space. Their hands and feet, if they are shown at all, are small, stick-like, and useless. One large figure with wings resembles an angel and others are accompanied by tiny bird or animal figures. The pictures are painted mostly in red pigments, made from iron oxide

Scholars often describe these otherworldly anthropomorphic figures as shamanic, suggesting that they depict supernatural transformations of shamans, who are accompanied by their spiritual guides or helpers. Shamans played, and still play, an important role as healers in pre-agricultural societies and a part of their practice involves leaving their physical form to make contact with supernatural powers beyond.

The panel appears on the face of a reddish sandstone cliff along the road, four miles above where Buckhorn Wash enters the San Rafael River. While easily accessible to view and photograph, a telephoto lens and binoculars are recommended. An interpretive sign at the site shows pictures of the panel before and after its restoration. You will need about half an hour to see the pictographs.

The San Rafael Swell, as this area is called, is a very scenic part of Utah. The Bureau of Land Management maintains an attractive rustic campground where the road crosses the San Rafael River. Overnight accommodations and travel services can be found in Price and Green River. The Museum of the San Rafael in Castle Dale has rock art and dinosaur exhibits. Here you also can obtain directions to the Rochester Creek Panel and other nearby rock art sites. The Cleveland Lloyd Dinosaur Quarry, located between this site and Price, makes another interesting stop.

Suggested reading: *Legacy on Stone,* by Sally J. Cole, Johnson Books, Boulder, 1990. Also, Southeastern Central Utah, Utah Multipurpose Map No. 2. This map (1/4 inch = 1 mile) will be useful as you explore this area.

## Sego Canyon Rock Art Site

*The Sego Canyon Rock Art Site is just north of Thompson, Utah. From Green River, follow Interstate 70 east for 25 miles to the Thompson Exit. Drive through this settlement across the railroad tracks and proceed 4 miles to the parking area at the site. Information: (435) 259-6111.*

The pictographs at Sego Canyon, like those at Buckhorn Wash, poignantly communicate the mystical dimension of Southwestern Archaic hunter-gatherer society. Here, at the junction of Sego and Thompson washes, two panels of pictures on sandstone cliffs contain impressive groupings of anthropomorphs thought to be from the late Archaic period. Anthropologists believe paintings like these were executed by shamans during or following trance states in which they would come in contact with supernatural beings. From these experiences, they would gain powers needed to carry out healing and religious ceremonies. (For further discussion of this topic, please refer to the preceding chapter.)

The tall, broad-shouldered figures on the main panel are painted in reddish pigments. Most have long, curved horns or antennae and round, oversized, staring eyes, which resemble empty eye sockets. Absent arms and legs, their heavy trapezoidal bodies appear to float in

*Pictographs of tall elongated figures at Buckhorn Wash.*

*Archaic-period rock paintings at Sego Canyon.*

space. All these elements give the figures a spectral appearance. Of this rock art, author Polly Schaasfma has written, "Artists of the Barrier Canyon Anthropomorphic Style focused primarily on the emotional impact of their work." If this is true, those at Sego Canyon certainly succeeded.

What is extraordinary about the Sego site is that in addition to the Barrier Canyon-style paintings, it also includes a separate large panel of Fremont petroglyphs and another panel with Ute pictographs. The Fremonters pecked pictures of triangle-shaped human figures wearing elaborate headdresses and necklaces with pendants. As in the Archaic panel, these anthropomorphs are lacking arm and leg appendages. Also included in the panel are numerous fat-bodied bighorn sheep and other designs.

The Ute Indians were living as hunter-gatherers in this region when the Spanish first settled New Mexico in the late sixteenth century. After around 1700, the Utes came in possession of horses, which allowed them to greatly expand their hunting territory. Their relationship with their neighbors also changed, and by the mid-1700s, they were raiding Navajo, Spanish, and Pueblo settlements with impunity. The Ute pictograph panel, which probably dates to the late eighteenth or early nineteenth century, features two imposing, standing human figures as well as several others mounted on horseback. There also are horses and buffaloes and two huge round white shields decorated in red. As a whole, the panel has a bold, "in-your-face" feeling.

The rock art at Sego Canyon suffered badly at the hands of vandals but recently was restored by a professional rock art conservator. The Bureau of Land Management built a parking area, landscaped the site with pathways and rail fences, and installed interpretive signs. There are picnic tables here, too.

Thompson is a tiny settlement that appears to have seen more prosperous days. Its sole cafe was a set in the popular movie, *Thelma and Louise*. The nearest towns with travel services are Green River and Moab.

*Jornada Mogollon cave painting of the Rain God,*
*Tlaloc, at Hueco Tanks State Historical Park.*

# The Mogollon
## Roots of Pueblo Culture

P ueblo culture in the Southwest has its roots among a people of shadowy origins who seemingly vanished long before Europeans arrived in North America. They are called the Mogollon (mug-ee-yone), named for a range of mountains in their culture area, which in turn, are named for a seventeenth-century New Mexican governor.

The Mogollon lived in small settlements in the wooded, well-watered highlands that curve down from the upper tributaries of the Little Colorado River. They ranged through the southern Arizona–New Mexico border country and further south to below Casas Grandes (p. 26) in Mexico. One Mogollon branch, the Mimbres, lived in the region surrounding present-day Silver City and Deming, New Mexico; and another, the Jornada, survived in the desert country to the east. Examples of their rock art can be seen at Three Rivers (p. 21) and Hueco Tanks (p. 23).

Mogollon origins have been traced to Archaic period hunter-gatherers—often referred to as the Cochise Culture—who roamed this broad country on their seasonal rounds for thousands of years. About three thousand years ago, these seminomadic people began to tend fields of corn, establish settled communities, and adopt other practices that archaeologists identify as Mogollon.

Initially, the Mogollon placed their villages on high ground. Later, they settled closer to their cultivated fields in the valleys. Their family dwelling was the pithouse, a small round or oblong structure built over a shallow excavation with low slab-lined walls and a hard dirt floor in which cists were dug for storage. Interior upright posts supported roof timbers that were often raised in a conical formation and overlaid with sticks, grasses, and a layer of dirt. Villages often consisted of fifteen or twenty pithouses, one of which usually was larger and used for community functions.

The Mogollon started to use ceramic containers instead of baskets for cooking and seed storage. Being nonperishable, pottery would later prove to be of great value to archaeologists, who analyze design styles, which changed over space and time. Mimbres potters—the Mimbres were a branch of the Mogollon—decorated their ceramics with exquisitely painted birds, animals, fish, people, mythic figures, and abstract designs. This artistic tradition provides a view into their world. So fascinating are Mimbres bowls that soon after their first discovery an illicit international trade developed. Regrettably, this has resulted in the wholesale looting of most Mimbres sites.

Sometime after A.D. 900, the Mogollon came to be strongly influenced by the expansive Anasazi-Pueblo culture centered on the Colorado Plateau to the north. This influence is apparent in the aboveground masonry architecture of Casa Malpais (p. 28) and the cliff dwellings at Gila Cliffs (p. 19). But the Mogollon also had ties to the south, especially with the dynamic trading center at Casas Grandes, Mexico.

You may wonder why this guidebook includes so few Mogollon sites to visit. The reason is that most of the Mogollon structures were built of perishable materials, such as wood and mud. After a few years of weathering, they melted back into the earth. The remains of a Mogollon pithouse village could conceivably be reconstructed, but if done authentically, it too would soon decompose. Although pithouses don't quite beguile the imagination as do cliff dwellings, we should not forget the contributions the Mogollon made to the evolution of farming and human culture in the Southwest.

Suggested reading: *Mogollon,* by Rose Houk, Southwest Parks and Monuments Association, Tucson, Arizona, 1992.

*Sketch of Mogollon pithouse.*

*Mogollon cliff dwelling at Gila Cliffs.*

# Gila Cliff Dwellings

*Gila Cliff Dwellings are located at the end of New Mexico 15, 44 miles (1.5 hours driving time) north of Silver City, in southwestern New Mexico. Information: (505) 536-9461. Entrance fee.*

It comes as a surprise to find Mogollon dwellings closely resembling the cliff houses of the Anasazi, but such is the case at Gila Cliff Dwellings National Monument. How did this come about? The question has intrigued researchers.

Cultures, like people, tend to influence their neighbors. By the 1200s, the ancestral Puebloans of the Four Corners region had expanded far beyond their original boundaries, carrying with them many ideas, including how to build. As archaeologists reconstruct the history of Gila Cliff Dwellings, Mogollon folk living some forty miles to the west, near present-day Reserve, New Mexico, moved to Gila Cliffs to build their new dwellings in the cliff-house style of their northern neighbors.

Dates obtained from original roof timbers show that these dwellings were built in the 1270s or 1280s, probably by a dozen or so families, and remained in use until around A.D. 1300. The inhabitants raised crops on the mesas and cultivated garden plots along portions of the streambeds. Like all prehistoric Southwestern Indians, they also subsisted by collecting a variety of plants and seeds, hunting game, and trading with neighboring communities for other supplies and commodities they wanted.

At Gila Cliffs, you should pick up a trail guide at the visitor center before going to the trailhead, which is just over a mile away. The mile-long path crosses the West Fork of the Gila River, winds up Cliff Dwellers Canyon, and loops back to the caves. In the shade of tall pines, this scenic walk initially follows the creek, then leads into some steeper climbing. You can explore many of the more than forty well-preserved rooms elevated 150 feet above the creek in deeply recessed caves. Despite looting and vandalism by early American settlers and miners, the stone masonry walls are well preserved. From the cliff dwellings, the trail returns by a different route to the river and parking area. You should plan at least forty-five minutes for the tour and longer for a more leisurely sightseeing experience.

In the late 1800s, this country was a stronghold of the Chiricahua Apaches, some of whose leaders—Mangas Coloradas, Cochise, Victorio, and Geronimo, for example—became legendary figures of Indian resistance to Euro-American expansion in the Southwest. In 1884, Adolph F. Bandelier came here during his famed archaeological explorations of the Southwest and described these ruins in his journals.

Gila Cliff Dwellings are contained within a 533-acre preserve managed jointly by the National Park Service and the National Forest Service. More than three million acres of wilderness surround the monument to comprise one of the Southwest's most beautiful and primitive regions. With over two thousand miles of trails, the Gila Wilderness is a paradise for hikers, backpackers, and packtrippers. One can roam this area for weeks and only meet a few other souls.

A Forest Service campground is maintained near Gila Cliff Dwellings and gas, food, camping supplies, lodging, horse rentals, and guided pack trips are available at nearby Gila Hot Springs. The historic mining town of Silver City offers a wide choice of travel services. You can visit several interesting sites in the Silver City area, including historic houses, Fort Bayard, and the old mining camp of Pinos Altos.

Suggested reading: *Gila Cliff Dwellings National Monument,* by Laurence Parent, Southwest Parks and Monuments Association, Tucson, Arizona, 1992.

*Petroglyph of a bighorn sheep at Three Rivers.*

# Three Rivers Petroglyph Site

*At Three Rivers, an intersection along U.S. 54, 30 miles north of Alamogordo, New Mexico, turn east and proceed for 5 miles to the entrance to the Three Rivers Petroglyph Site parking lot. From here, one trail leads through the petroglyph area and another to excavated ruins. Information: (505) 525-4300. Entrance fee.*

Rock art sites are widely scattered throughout areas of the Southwest where Native Americans lived, traveled, hunted, drew water, maintained shrines, or gathered together for religious and social purposes. Much rock art, however, is located in remote places or on private property and, while known to archaeologists and local folk, is virtually unknown to the general public. While erosion and vandalism has taken its toll over the passing centuries, many sites have endured in remarkably fine condition.

Petroglyphs (from the Greek petros, "stone," and glyphe, "carving") are images that have been pecked, chiseled, grooved, or scratched on rock surfaces. Most were executed by striking a hard stone against the surface of a boulder or cliff, thus removing the darkened patina or desert varnish to expose the lighter undersurface. To gain greater control, hammer and chisel stones often were used. Techniques and styles varied greatly and while some inscriptions seem to be no more than doodling, others exhibit remarkable sophistication.

The Three Rivers Petroglyph Site contains one of the largest collections of rock art in the Southwest. Here, some twenty thousand glyphs were pecked on boulders scattered across more than fifty acres along a ridge near the western base of the Sacramento Mountains. The pictures depict animals, birds, fish, reptiles, insects, and plants, as well as geometric and abstract designs. Anthropomorphic forms and masks can be found as well.

These petroglyphs are thought to have been made between A.D. 900 and 1400 by Jornada Mogollon people who lived in this desert region. The remains of a Mogollon pithouse village, is located only about two hundred yards south of the petroglyph ridge. An interpretive trail leads to this partially excavated site. Viewers will recognize similarities of style and content between many of these petroglyphs and the paintings found on contemporaneous Mimbres Mogollon ceramics. The heart of the Mimbres region lies in hill country a hundred miles to the west of Three Rivers.

The Three Rivers site has a stunning view over the arid Tularosa Basin. Exploring this site can be a sweltering experience in the summer and you would be well advised to wear a sun hat and bring a water bottle. Weather conditions permitting, you should plan to spend at least an hour at this site; you may decide to stay longer to hike, explore, and ponder the significance of the images.

Three Rivers is a quiet and peaceful place; however, as you absorb its atmosphere, remember that not far across the desert to the east, in the early morning hours of July 16, 1945, an awesome explosion occurred at another site called Trinity.

Next to the parking area, you will find picnic tables, barbecue pits, drinking water, and toilets. Overnight camping is permitted. A National Forest Service campground is located several miles further up the road, and travel facilities are available in the towns of Alamogordo and Carrizozo. Other nearby points of interest are White Sands National Monument and the historic town of Lincoln.

Suggested reading: *Archaeological Survey, Three Rivers Drainage, New Mexico,* by Mark Wimberly and Alan Rogers, El Paso Archaeological Society, El Paso, Texas, 1977.

*Painted masks believed to represent Quetzalcoatl at Hueco Tanks.*

# Hueco Tanks State Historical Park

*Hueco Tanks State Historical Park is located 32 miles northeast of El Paso, Texas. From El Paso, drive 24 miles east on U.S. 62/180, then turn north on Ranch Road 2775 and continue 8 miles to the park's entrance. Information: (915) 857-1135. Entrance fee.*

Hueco Tanks, a series of rocky hills and water traps, has been a magnet to human beings for some twelve thousand years. Today, the area is best known for its extraordinary collection of ancient Indian rock paintings, or pictographs, which offer a glimpse into the minds and spirits of Native Americans who lived or camped here over many centuries.

The setting for the pictographs—there are some petroglyphs, too—are three volcanic outcrops, the weathered remnants of a magma dome that rose close to the earth's surface in the distant geologic past. While the magma never erupted here as a volcano, it eventually was exposed when the overlying geologic layers were worn away by erosion. After rains, water here drains off the rocky slopes to collect in natural catchments or cisterns, popularly called "tanks." Some additional large tanks were made by ranchers in the twentieth century. The Spanish word, *hueco*, meaning hole, or hollow, refers to the many natural cup-like depressions in the rock surface that also hold rain water.

The first indigenous people to place markings on the rocks in the Hueco Tanks area were seminomadic hunter-gatherers in the period of the Western Archaic or Desert Culture (6000 B.C. to A.D. 450). Early on, they emphasized abstract motifs such as circles, dots, zigzags, and parallel wavy lines in their rock writings, but after around 3000 B.C., they incorporated human-like and animal figures and hunting scenes. The anthropomorphic figures have some of the attributes (broad shoulders, horned headdresses, small heads, and appendages) that characterize Archaic rock art in southeastern Utah and south Texas, suggesting widespread cultural commonalities.

What has made Hueco Tanks so well known as a rock art locale, however, are the finely executed masks painted by Indians of the Jornada Mogollon culture, probably in the 1100s and 1200s. Both linear and solidly painted masks are found here on the walls and ceilings of rock shelters and caves. The predominant color is a faded red, though black, white, brown, green, and various shades of ocher (an earthly yellow or red) also were used. The linear masks show an outlined head with facial features and headdress. The solid masks, on the other hand, depict only the painted mask with empty or negative spaces left for the eyes. Thus, the person or spirit behind the mask is left to your imagination. The skillfully painted solid masks are characterized by horizontal bands of color, giving them an abstract quality. Many are found in deep, dark recesses where they have remained well preserved.

Scholars have identified representations of two Mesoamerican deities among the Mogollon masks at Hueco Tanks. One is the Rain God known as Tlaloc (p. 16). This hideous figure is characterized by a large trapezoidal head that sits atop a chunky, armless torso with decorative elements. Tlaloc is especially recognizable by its large goggle eyes that stare vacantly and disturbingly out at you. The masks at Hueco Tanks also include representations of Quetzalcoatl, the multifaceted Mexican deity, who can assume the form of a plumed or horned head with a serpent's body. In the Cave of the Masks, the feathered plume or curved horn appears as a bent-over conical hat.

Members of the buffalo-hunting tribes of the Southern Plains, including Apaches, Comanches, and Kiowas, used Hueco Tanks as a campsite, especially in the eighteenth and nineteenth centuries when they ranged over extensive territories on horseback. Rock art from these groups also can be seen in rock shelters and caves of Hueco Tanks. One intensely vandalized site near the visitor center has a large petroglyph of a costumed figure, and Comanche Cave contains a large decorated shield pictograph and panels showing lines of dancers.

In the 1970s, archaeologists conducted test excavations in the flats near the base of the hills. The site they selected had no visible architecture, but it had an abundance of artifacts lying on the ground. They unearthed a series of pithouses, which they attributed to the Doña Ana phase of the Jornada Mogollon culture, dating from between around A.D. 1150 to 1300. It is assumed that additional archaeological surveys and tests would reveal more Mogollon hamlets in the area. Presumably, it was these part-time farmers who were responsible for the masks, Tlaloc figures, and other Mogollon-era pictographs, as well as a number of prehistoric ditches and water diversion features that have been recorded.

Of particular historical interest are the remains of an Overland Mail Company station along the famous Butterfield Trail. This romantic 2,795-mile-long mail route, which ran between St. Louis and San Francisco, began operation in September, 1858, but was discontinued at the outbreak of the Civil War in 1861. Coaches carried passengers as well as mail on the arduous trip, which took just under three weeks. After enduring rough terrain, extreme weather conditions, and threats from hostile Indians, rest and supply stops such as the station here were a welcome sight, indeed. The station remains are next to the park's visitor center.

Much of the pleasure you will experience on a visit to Hueco Tanks lies in the area's unusual geology and beautiful natural environment. In a desert region with an annual rainfall of about eight inches, this one-by two-mile park is like an oasis; in fact, you could skip the rock art altogether and still be richly rewarded by the rocks, water holes, lush vegetation, and animal and bird life.

Hueco Tanks State Historical Park emphasizes education and preservation in its public programs. Your experience will begin with an orientation on the area's natural and cultural history and rock art preservation guidelines. Park interpretive staff lead several guided walking tours, which are rated from easy to strenuous and take from an hour

Pictograph of shield in Comanche Cave.

and a half to six hours. With advance planning, a customized guided tour also can be arranged. The major part of the park is accessible only with a guide. Call well in advance to make arrangements or to join a regularly scheduled tour.

Camping is available in the park, but you must call at least two weeks in advance for a reservation. The nearest motels, restaurants, and grocery stores are along routes 62/180 on the east side of El Paso.

Suggested reading: *Rock Paintings at Hueco Tanks State Historical Park,* by Kay Sutherland, Texas Parks and Wildlife Department, Austin, Texas, 1995.

# Casas Grandes

*The ruins of Casas Grandes (Paquimé) are located just outside Casas Grandes, Chihuahua, Mexico, approximately 180 miles southwest of Ciudad Juarez, Chihuahua, and El Paso, Texas, along Mexico 2. Entrance fee.*

Just south of the New Mexico–Mexico border lie the monumental ruins of Casas Grandes, a prehistoric Indian city whose influence extended throughout its immediate region and the American Southwest. Some of the technological and commercial achievements of Casas Grandes' inhabitants surpassed those of the contemporaneous Mogollon, Hohokam, or Anasazi cultures to the north.

Casas Grandes is located in a broad, well-watered valley in the northern Chihuahua desert. The region's basin-and-range topography, which provided a variety of resources to support the city, extends unbroken into southern New Mexico and Arizona, with whose prehistoric inhabitants the Casas Grandes people maintained active cultural and economic links.

Much of Casas Grandes' core city, Paquimé, was excavated between 1958 and 1961 by the Amerind Foundation of Dragoon, Arizona, under the direction of the late Charles C. Di Peso. The Foundation later published the results of this research in a series of volumes, including an informative summary by Di Peso.

Construction of Paquimé's multistoried, rammed-earth buildings began sometime after A.D. 1250. Di Peso argued that the city was ruled by a group of entrepreneurs, who represented Mesoamerican trading guilds far to the south. Recognizing Casas Grandes' potential as a commercial base, these puchtecas forged local support into political power to eventually dominate a vast area of what is now northwestern Chihuahua and northeastern Sonora. Di Peso liked to compare their trading empire, which reached hundreds of miles to the north, to that of the later Hudson Bay Company in Canada. Cadres of traders and a network of trading posts brought materials and ideas across great dis-

*Ruins of Paquimé at Casas Grandes.*

tances, connecting culturally disparate societies. Prime trade items included parrots, feathers, copper bells, sea shells, and turquoise.

Paquimé's commercial success spurred population growth and extensive urban renewal. Large marketplaces with warehousing facilities were built, as well as ceremonial mounds, ballcourts, plazas, and a complex of apartment buildings. Di Peso speculated that Paquimé's brilliance drew multitudes of visitors from the hinterlands to further "fill the larders of the city and its masters." He also saw a linkage between Paquimé and Chaco Canyon, a connection now advocated by archaeologist Stephen H. Lekson in his 1998 book, *The Chaco Meridian*.

As Casas Grandes gained power and influence, its rulers probably recruited a local work force to construct a sophisticated domestic water system. The water source was a spring, Ojo Vareleño, northwest of the city, which still gushes more than three thousand gallons per minute. Aqueducts brought this flow to a reservoir where it was dispersed in under-ground stone-lined channels to the main house clusters. Other system features included drainage tunnels and subterranean walk-in cisterns.

Paquimé's elite enjoyed other benefits such as heated sleeping platforms, airy living room spaces, raised-platform cooking hearths, and city parks. Aviculture, evidenced by the remains of turkey and macaw pens along the edge of plazas, became a lucrative and prestigious part of the economy.

Sometime after A.D. 1400, civil construction ceased and Casas Grandes' once-impressive buildings began to fall into disrepair. The good times were over. Did trading problems cause the economic slump? Or was it drought, or a popular revolt? To date, archaeology has revealed no definitive answer. Whatever happened, when European explorers first entered Casas Grandes' domain more than a century later, they found the city in ruins and the valley deserted.

Thanks to the region's arid climate, the massiveness of Paquimé's adobe buildings, and stabilization work by the Mexican government, this archaeological site offers much to marvel at. You will gain a sense of the power Casas Grandes once enjoyed. A handsome new on-site museum containing Casas Grandes' artifacts augments the experience of exploring the ruins.

To complement a visit to the ruins of Paquimé, a stroll around the historic plaza of the nearby town of Casas Grandes will help you to appreciate present-day Mexican life and culture and perhaps even to catch the ambiance of Hispanic New Mexican villages a century ago. You will find motels, restaurants, and other travel services in the nearby modern city of Nuevo Casas Grandes. The highways to Columbus, New Mexico, and El Paso, Texas, are well marked and in good condition.

Suggested reading: *Casas Grandes: A Fallen Trading Post of the Gran Chichimeca*, 3 vols., by Charles C. Di Peso, Northland Press, Flagstaff, Arizona, 1974.

# Casa Malpais

*Casa Malpais ruins, on the west side of Springerville, Arizona, off U.S. 60, are accessible only by guided tour. The Casa Malpais Visitor Center, at 318 West Main Street, conducts tours every day at 9 and 11 A.M. and 2:30 P.M., weather permitting. (Check in advance to confirm this schedule.) Arrive before departure times to register and see to the museum. Information: (520) 333-2123. Entrance fee.*

Casa Malpais, or "badlands house," is true to its name. This Mogollon site is located along the edge of an eroded lava flow above the Little Colorado River in east-central Arizona. The fracturing and slumping of the lava cliffs tens of thousands of years ago created a series of narrow terraces upon which the ancient village was built of black basaltic rocks in the late 1200s.

A unique aspect of Casa Malpais is its volcanic environs. A vast lava

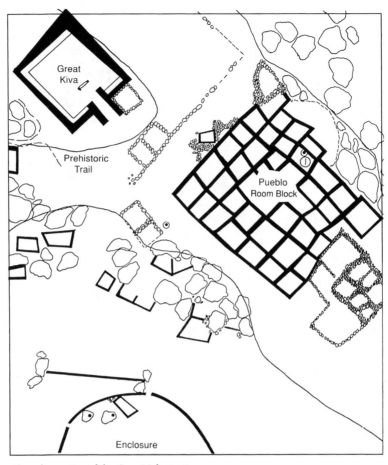

*Plan of a portion of the Casa Malpais site.*
*Courtesy Louis Berger & Associates, Inc.*

plain extends to the north and old cinder cones dot the landscape to the north and west. To the south and east lies Round Valley, a scenic basin at seven thousand foot elevation, used historically by sheepherders and horse thieves. In the early and late light of the day, the sun's rays rake over this unusual terrain sprinkled with grazing horses and cattle.

Mogollon Indian settlers established pithouse villages in this region as early as A.D. 700 and two hundred years later their population was on the increase. By A.D. 1100, perhaps taking a clue from their nearby Anasazi neighbors, they had begun building above-ground masonry pueblos. Casa Malpais thrived until sometime after A.D. 1400, when Mogollon culture in general fizzled. The Hopi and Zuni Indians claim affinity to this site and are consulted regarding archaeological and management issues.

Along the interpretive trail, which is just under a mile in length, you will skirt along the edge of a large flat area on the first terrace from

*View of the great kiva at Casa Malpais.*

which all stones and boulders were long ago removed. This cleared field may have been used by large gatherings of people as a camping ground, for trade fairs, or for ritual events. The next feature you will see is quite remarkable—a huge square kiva whose massive rock walls still stand over six feet high in places.

The trail wends over a 120-room house mound, which was being excavated in the late 1990s, and ascends through a modified fissure to the top of the mesa. At this high point, you will have a sweeping view over the site and landscape. On the return walk, you will see the remains of several small residential compounds and an unusual large stone-walled oval that has five openings. Some have speculated that it once functioned as an astronomical observatory.

Still another unique aspect of Casa Malpais are its catacombs. These sacred chambers, which lie in deep crevices, once contained an estimated two hundred burials, most of which were looted over the years. Because they are hazardous to enter, they are not open to the public.

In the late 1600s, this region was inhabited by nomadic Apaches, who took advantage of the rich hunting and foraging along the Little Colorado River. European-American settlers, attracted by the region's

fine stock-grazing potential, arrived in the late nineteenth century. As the town of Springerville developed, Casa Malpais began to suffer from vandalism and looting. Even so, the site as a whole remains remarkably intact and is a source of much interest to researchers and visitors. It is well worth the drive from Interstate 40 to see this archaeological preserve.

Apart from archaeological surveys and testing, Casa Malpais was not seriously investigated until the 1990s, when a program of systematic excavations was begun. An interesting collection of artifacts from the site, including pottery, jewelry, stone tools, and yucca sandals, is on view at the visitor center in Springerville. Here, you can also buy craft items and books.

Springerville has gas stations, restaurants, and lodging. Other nearby archaeological sites are Homol'ovi Ruins State Park (p. 106) and Petrified Forest National Park (p. 109). In addition, from spring through fall, Lyman Lake State Park offers boat tours to see petroglyphs along the lake shore. For further information, call (520) 337-4441.

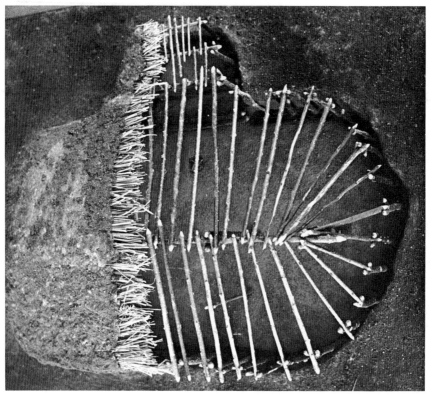

*Cut-away model of Hohokam house.*

# The Hohokam
## Ancient Dwellers of the Desert

C entered in the Phoenix Basin of south-central Arizona, the Hohokam were a seminal Southwestern culture with widespread influence. They are remembered especially for their construction of some five hundred miles of canals, the building of ballcourts and platform mounds, and the manufacture of finely crafted jewelry, pottery, and mosaics. In addition, they developed a widespread trading network that extended far beyond their homeland.

Most archaeologists are of the opinion that the Hohokam had a local hunter-gatherer origin. More than three thousand years ago, seminomadic foragers, who had long roamed the southern deserts, began to adopt a more settled agricultural life and to produce a plain polished redware style of pottery. As their population increased and their society grew more complex, they acquired cultural attributes that archaeologists designate as "Hohokam."

One remarkable accomplishment of the Hohokam was the building of a vast network of irrigation canals. The main canals, some of which are fifty feet wide at the bottom, fed hundreds of smaller ditches that brought water to thousands of acres of croplands. The Hohokam established villages at regular intervals along the main canals, creating a complex, interlocking social and economic system that, more than anything else, explains the success of their long-lived society. Through their organizational and engineering skills, combined with a deep pool of human labor, they brought water to the desert and produced agricultural surpluses for export.

Although the common folk lived in simple dwellings built of mud and sticks, Hohokam communities built large-scale public structures, such as ballcourts, over two hundred of which have been found in

*Hohokam-style ballcourt at Wupatki National Monument.*

Arizona. Oval in form, they ranged from seventy-five feet long by forty-five feet wide to nearly triple that size. Within this sunken arena, it is thought, contestants played a ritual game that had sacred as well as sportive overtones. The game, as witnessed by early Spaniards in Mexico, involved knocking a rubber ball up and down the court and through stone hoops, using only the hips and arms. You can see examples of ballcourts at Pueblo Grande Ruins (p. 36) and Wupatki National Monument (p. 148).

Large earthen platform mounds at the center of villages represent another form of Hohokam monumental architecture, especially after A.D. 1100. The mounds were surrounded by clusters of houses within adobe compound walls. Fifty village sites have such mounds, some of which contain as many as thirty-two thousand cubic yards of fill and are topped by small temple ruins. The best example is at Pueblo Grande. Rituals and dances to please the gods probably were held on the mounds at certain times of the year. Around A.D. 1300, residences began to be built on top of the mounds, suggesting the appearance of an elite or affluent merchant class of people.

The Hohokam were highly skilled craftspeople producing a fine red-on-buff style of pottery and a variety of figurines and masks. They fashioned paint pallets, bowls, censers, and a variety of stone tools and weapons. They also excelled in the production of shell ornaments, such as beads, rings, bracelets, and pendants. The shells were imported from the Gulf of California, then etched by artisans using an acid solution made from fermented saguaro juice. This was a uniquely Hohokam art form.

While we are inclined to praise cultures for their material creations, such as art and architecture, we have only to drive into the Sonoran Desert in summer to realize the Hohokams' chief accomplishment—survival in a most challenging environment. The Hohokams' knowledge of their desert world, combined with an innovative approach to dealing with heat and aridity, allowed their culture to prosper. They harnessed the region's precious water resources to successfully cultivate corn, beans, squash, cotton, and agave. They harvested wild plants with nutritious or healing qualities, collected cactus fruits, and hunted birds and mammals. Although archaeological evidence shows an end to Hohokam culture around A.D. 1450, it is widely believed that such tribes as the Pima and Tohono O'Odham (Papago) are their genetic descendants. This assumption is based on native oral traditions as well as archaeological and historical clues. Besides, it was these tribes whom Spanish explorers met in colonial times and who inhabit the ancient Hohokam world today.

Suggested reading: *The Hohokam: Ancient People of the Desert,* edited by David Grant Noble, School of American Research Press, Santa Fe, New Mexico, 1991.

*Ceramic figurines excavated from Pueblo Grande in Phoenix.*

# Pueblo Grande Ruins

*Pueblo Grande Ruins are located at the Pueblo Grande Museum, 4619 East Washington Street (corner of 44th Street) in Phoenix, Arizona. From Interstate 10, take the Hohokam Expressway or 48th Street exit northbound. Information: (602) 495-0901. Entrance fee.*

The Salt River, which rises in the White Mountains of east-central Arizona, flows through Roosevelt Reservoir in the Tonto Basin to water the broad agricultural flatlands around Phoenix. Along its north bank, near the Sky Harbor International Airport, lies a partially excavated Hohokam village that was first occupied nearly fifteen hundred years ago. Pueblo Grande was one of the largest of about fifty Hohokam settlements whose remains presently lie beneath Phoenix.

At its peak in the 1300s, Pueblo Grande probably covered a two-square-mile area. At that time, it was comprised of many residential compounds, a "big house" similar to Casa Grande (p. 41), a twenty-foot-high platform mound as big as a football field and covered with houses, a couple ballcourts, and hundreds of small dwellings composed of sticks and mud. The village was situated at the headwaters of a major canal system, which irrigated extensive fields of corn, beans, squash, and cotton. When Hohokam society collapsed in the 1400s, Pueblo Grande became part of the mythology of the Pima Indians, who still live nearby.

In the last century, Euro-American settlers discovered the rich agricultural potential of the Phoenix Basin and put the Pueblo Grande area under cultivation to produce cotton. Even the three-story big house was razed, its bulk used as fill to level fields. The huge platform mound, however, was spared because it contained too much stone to make leveling feasible. It is this feature and the adjacent ballcourt that are the surviving components of Pueblo Grande today.

Although construction of the mound probably took place over a two hundred-year period, one researcher estimates that it would have taken a hundred people twenty-four months to complete. Retained by a massive wall consisting of hardened chunks of caliche and river rocks, it contains thirty-two thousand cubic yards of fill. Houses and other specialized structures stood both on and around it to form a residential and ceremonial compound that was itself walled in. Who lived in this special area within the larger Pueblo Grande town? Possibly an elite or priestly class of people who derived their power from control and management of the canals and success as traders and merchants. The size and prominence of their dwellings would have reflected their status.

At Pueblo Grande, one cannot help but be impressed by the stark contrast between the pre-Columbian ruins and the modern city. As we watch cars, freight trains, and jumbo jets moving over this ancient site,

*View from above the Pueblo Grande platform mound in Phoenix, showing modern canals, railroad train, highway, and airport in distance.*

we are reminded of the ephemeral nature of culture and civilization.

Since Adolph F. Bandelier first visited Pueblo Grande in 1883, many archaeologists have probed the secrets of this site. Between 1988 and 1990, Soil Systems, Inc. excavated portions of the town to the north and east of the museum, which lay in the easement of the planned Hohokam Expressway. During the course of this work, extensive ruins from the Classic period (A.D. 1100–1450) were uncovered and later reported on. At about the same time, the Pueblo Grande Museum published a synthesis of a century of research at the site, gleaned from archived field notes and unpublished reports.

The Pueblo Grande Museum, which is adjacent to the platform mound, contains exhibits relating to the Hohokam and other past and present-day Indian cultures of southern Arizona. From the museum, an interpretive trail leads to the mound, excavated rooms, and a restored ball court. You can also view nearby prehistoric and modern canals.

One wonders, of course, what happened to the Hohokam of Pueblo Grande. Archaeologists look to a possible social breakdown or the destruction of the canal system from floods. The Pima Indians, however, have another explanation, passed down from person to person over the centuries. They say that long ago the Sivanyi (Hohokam) offended the Pima's hero, Elder Brother, and even tried to kill him. In retaliation, the Pima and Tohono O'Odham Indians made war upon them and destroyed the Sivanyi villages, including Casa Grande (p. 41) and Pueblo Grande. Perhaps one day the Pima legend will be substantiated by archaeological findings.

The Pueblo Grande Museum, which was founded in the 1920s, is open daily and periodically conducts special interpretive programs and field trips. Restaurants and hotels can be found within walking distance. While here, you may also wish to visit the Park of the Canals (below) in Mesa and the Heard Museum in Phoenix, which has extensive Native American collections.

Suggested reading: *Desert Farmers at the River's Edge: The Hohokam and Pueblo Grande,* by John P. Andrews and Todd W. Bostwick, City of Phoenix, Phoenix, Arizona, 1997.

# Park of the Canals

*The Park of the Canals is located at 1710 N. Horne Street, between McKellips Road and Brown Street, in Mesa, Arizona. The park, which includes a botanical garden as well as old canals, is open daily. Information: (602) 827-4700.*

The Hohokam Indians, masters of irrigation agriculture, constructed extensive canal systems from rivers along which they built their villages and tilled their fields. In the Salt River Valley alone, archaeologists have recorded hundreds of miles of ancient canals, many of which were modified for continued use in the nineteenth and twentieth centuries. By A.D. 1000, Hohokam canals are believed to have watered more than 110,000 acres and sustained a population of thirty thousand to sixty thousand people.

All but a small fraction of the Hohokam canals have disappeared due to modern development and urbanization. To our good fortune, however, private preservationists and the Mesa Archaeological and Historical Society purchased and set aside land with canal sites in the Mesa area. Now these canals are part of a municipal park.

*University of Arizona archaeologist, Emil Haury, standing in
a freshly excavated Hohokam canal at Snaketown. Courtesy
Arizona State Museum, photo by Helga Teiwes.*

Farming was the basis for Hohokam culture, which thrived for a millennium prior to around A.D. 1450. The Hohokam grew vegetables and grain as well as large quantities of cotton, which became an important export crop. Their trade network extended south into Mexico, west to the Pacific Coast, north to the Anasazi world, and east to the land of the Mogollon. Many researchers believe that the success of Hohokam agricultural enterprises gave rise to a ruling class, whose members were responsible for building the "big houses" and platform mounds for which this culture is noted.

A typical Hohokam canal system consisted of a main ditch stemming from a major waterway such as the Salt or Gila rivers. A network of tributary ditches, decreasing in size probably to the width of a shovel,

*The ruins of Casa Grande.*

branched off to water fields and garden plots. The main canals, which could reach a dozen miles in length and fifteen feet in depth, often linked a series of communities. One such canal was excavated at the Snaketown site near Phoenix in 1964. To function effectively, canal systems had to be well managed, which required a centralized administration. Water-control management, thus, helped form the structure of Hohokam society.

At the Park of the Canals, you will see the remains of several actual canals, which are now partially filled in and eroded. A footbridge crosses over one from the parking area. Remember that the Hohokam had only wooden digging sticks and baskets to move huge quantities of dirt.

Another canal, located immediately west of the botanical garden, was used in the 1870s by Mormon pioneers, who restored an ancient Hohokam canal. Still another is modern and remains in active use.

The Hohokam drew their canal water from the Salt River, which today is bone dry most of the time, its waters stored in Roosevelt Reservoir upstream to be released into modern canals rather than into the river bed. Still, when the reservoir occasionally fills up and spills over, downstream residents can see their old river flow again.

You will want about half an hour to see the Park of the Canals, including its botanical gardens. Restaurants and travel services can be found along McKellips Road. To learn more about the Hohokam of the Phoenix area, be sure to visit the Pueblo Grande Museum (p. 36).

# Casa Grande Ruins National Monument

*Casa Grande Ruins National Monument is located off Arizona 87/287, 1 mile north of Coolidge, Arizona. This is about midway between Phoenix and Tucson. Information: (520) 723-3172. Entrance fee.*

Casa Grande is a massive pueblo-style building on an open plain that has withstood the effects of weather and vandalism for six centuries. Its very existence today as more than just a dirt mound in the desert testifies to the strength of this "big house" and the immense construction investment of its builders.

The Hohokam Indians, who built this three-story mansion in the 1300s, designed it as a perfect 3:4 rectangle oriented to the cardinal directions. Deeply trenched in the ground, its walls are more than four feet thick at their base, tapering to two feet at full height. The building material was caliche-adobe mud, which was mixed to a thick consistency in pits in the ground, carried to the walls, and puddled by hand in courses about two-feet high. Evidence of these courses is still visible in the wall cracking. The caliche, a desert subsoil with high lime content, became brick-hard when it dried, which accounts for the fine preservation of these ruins.

*Hohokam jar, Casa Grande museum.*

Casa Grande's wood components included ponderosa pine, white fir, juniper, and mesquite. The heavier timbers—more than six hundred beams supported the ceilings—were carried here, or possibly floated down the Gila River, from mountainous regions fifty miles away. The Hohokam overlaid the beams with a decking of sticks, such as saguaro cactus ribs, covered by even finer grassy materials. Mud served as a final sealer.

The function of Casa Grande has long perplexed archaeologists. What was it? The literature is replete with speculations including a chief's residence, grain warehouse, temple, administrative center, and observatory for stargazers. Present researchers favor the view that a person of great influence—a chief or priest—lived here.

While technically four stories in height, the first story is actually a five-foot high base, which serves to elevate the structure. A high priest living here would have enjoyed a commanding view over residential compounds surrounding the big house and hundreds of mud huts beyond. The view over the canal system, whose intake was sixteen miles up the Gila River, may also have been relevant.

An intriguing feature of Casa Grande are several wall slots or portholes that appear to have a calendrical function. One on the single-room top floor aligns with the summer solstice sunset. Southwestern Indians, as we know from other sites and from historical accounts, devised systems like this to help predict important calendar days, such as when to plant and when to hold religious ceremonies.

The first European to lay eyes on Casa Grande, in 1694, was the Jesuit missionary, Eusebio Francisco Kino. Father Kino is renowned for the missions he built in southern Arizona and Sonora, Mexico. The ruins soon became a well-known landmark for explorers, travelers, soldiers, and pioneers. By 1880, the Southern Pacific Railroad, which had a station only twenty miles away, sponsored regular tours to view the site. In those days, Casa Grande had no more protection from souvenir hunters and vandals than it did from the weather, and many relics, including chunks of plaster and pieces of wood, were carried off.

National interest to protect Casa Grande began to crystalize following the 1887–1888 Hemenway Southwestern Archaeological Expedition, which included Frank H. Cushing, J. Walter Fewkes, Adolph F. Bandelier, and Frederick W. Hodge among its members. Four years later, Congress set aside 480 acres for the protection of the ruins and in 1903, a roof was erected over the big house.

Like all Classic-period (A.D. 1100 to 1450) Hohokam communities, Casa Grande saw a declining population in the 1300s and was abandoned in the mid-1400s. Theories abound, too, regarding the end of Hohokam culture. The Pima and Tohono O'Odham people tell of warfare. Archaeologists wonder about crop failures due to waterlogged or salinized soils, or a destructive flood, which eradicated canal systems. Whatever crisis befell the society, Casa Grande represents the pinnacle of Hohokam architecture and village planning.

An interpretive trail leads from the visitor center past the remains of an adobe pueblo, then to the big house, and on to the site of a ballcourt, where three hundred to six hundred spectators are believed to have gathered to watch this ritual sporting event. Park rangers also give guided tours. The monument has a small desert botanical garden, a picnic area, and a museum with displays of Hohokam craft arts and tools. You should plan to spend an hour or more to see the museum and ruins. Food and lodging are available in nearby Coolidge and Florence, and several campgrounds are located in the vicinity, although not at the monument itself.

Suggested reading: *Casa Grande Ruins National Monument,* by Rose Houk, Southwest Parks and Monuments Association, Tucson, Arizona, 1987.

# Painted Rocks Park

*Painted Rocks Park is located near Gila Bend, Arizona. From Gila Bend, drive 30 miles west on Interstate 8 to the Painted Rocks exit and continue another 15 miles to the park. Information: (623) 580-5500. Entrance fee.*

Painted Rocks Park contains one of the densest concentrations of petroglyphs in the Southwest. Long ago, Native Americans pecked more than 750 images on smooth-faced basalt boulders that cover an isolated hill in this otherwise flat country. Historical records indicate that some of the glyphs originally were painted, hence the site name.

The boulders at Painted Rocks are covered by an astounding array of pictures, including many human-like figures, animals, reptiles, and abstractions. Some images are of more recent origin, such as horses and riders. These later markings may have been made by Akimel O'Odham (Pima) or Tohono O'Odham (Papago) Indians, who are thought to be descendants of the Hohokam.

Why the Indians chose this place to draw their designs is a mystery. However, the boulder outcropping is a singular landmark along a trade route that probably was well traveled in ancient as well as modern times. In addition, these rocks, with their dark patina or desert varnish, seem to invite glyph making. Perhaps the site was a shrine or had special significance in the Indians' myths, and thus was a periodic gathering place for people living in the region.

Since there are no major habitation sites in the immediate vicinity of this petroglyph hill, archaeologists can only speculate as to the cultural affiliation of the glyph makers. The Gila Bend region, however, was within the Hohokam cultural domain from about A.D. 700 to 1450, and most of the glyphs are similar in style, the "Gila Petroglyph Style," to Hohokam rock art found to the east. (The remains of one Hohokam village, the Gatlin Site, is located just outside the town of Gila Bend. Since the town has plans to develop and interpret this site for visitors, you might check at the historical museum in town about its present status.) Archaeological studies show that after A.D. 1100, the Gila Bend area was influenced by the Patayan (ancestral Yuman) culture to the west, suggesting that for a period, at least, it was a contact zone between the Hohokam and Patayan peoples.

Until the Bureau of Land Management fenced off Painted Rocks in 1963, many of the smaller boulders with petroglyphs were carted off by people for front yard landscaping. The fencing, while unsightly, provides needed security and the site has seen little damage in recent years.

The nearest travel services are in the town of Gila Bend. You may also be interested in visiting Casa Grande Ruins National Monument (p. 41) near Coolidge.

*Petroglyphs on boulders at Painted Rocks Park.*

Suggested reading: "Hohokam, Patayan, or ?: Rock Art at Two Sites Near Gila Bend, Arizona," by Richard J. Martynec, *Rock Art Papers*, Vol. 6, edited by Ken Hedges, San Diego Museum Papers No. 24, San Diego, California, 1989.

# Romero Ruin

*The Romero Ruin is in Catalina State Park along Hwy. 77 (Oracle Road), 10 miles north of Tucson. The park's entrance is at milepost marker 81. Information: (520) 628-5798. Entrance fee.*

There are so few Hohokam archaeological sites that are open to the public that we are grateful when new ones, like the Romero Ruin, are developed and made available. Still, except for Casa Grande (p. 41), these sites tend to be subtle rather than spectacular monuments. At the Romero Ruin, you will see some remnants of a once-thriving village and learn about Hohokam prehistory in a beautiful desert setting. But there are no standing buildings or platform mounds here.

The Hohokam settled here along the western foothills of the Santa Catalina Mountains around A.D. 500 and stayed for about a thousand years. An initial small population built pithouses on the northern end

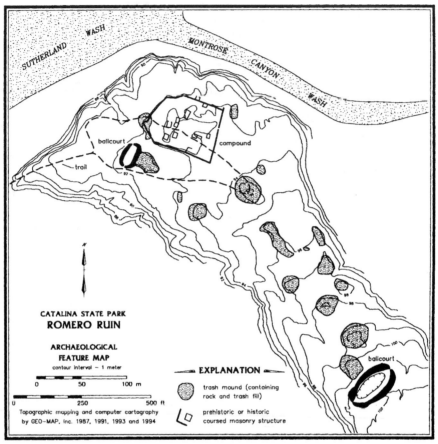

CATALINA STATE PARK
ROMERO RUIN

ARCHAEOLOGICAL
FEATURE MAP
contour interval — 1 meter

0        50        100 m

0        250        500 ft
Topographic mapping and computer cartography
by GEO-MAP, Inc. 1987, 1991, 1993 and 1994

⟶ EXPLANATION ⟵

trash mound (containing
rock and trash fill)

prehistoric or historic
coursed masonry structure

*Archaeological feature map of the Romero Ruin.*
*Courtesy Center for Desert Archaeology.*

of the ridge, close to Sutherland Wash, which then may have flowed
year around. The community's population reached a peak of an estimated three hundred people between A.D. 850 to 1000, then diminished until around A.D. 1450, when the last families moved away.

Archaeologists spent three field seasons investigating the Romero Ruin
between 1987 and 1993. Even so, only a portion of the fifteen-acre site was
excavated. Test pits dug in some of the trash mounds revealed much
information regarding how the ancient inhabitants lived, what they ate,
and with whom they traded. The remains of many stone tools and ceram
ic vessels helped to date the site and give clues to the diet of the Hohokam.
This included corn, squash, mesquite pods, agave, and paloverde seeds.
The numerous middens, or trash mounds, revealed the bones of deer,
bighorn sheep, antelopes, rabbits, quail, and reptiles. The archaeologists
also found marine shell artifacts, including bracelets crafted from
glycymeris shells from the Gulf of California, hundreds of miles distant.

A rock compound wall, originally six-feet high in places, once surrounded clusters of now-buried residential rooms. Between around A.D. 750 and 1000, the Hohokam built two ballcourts on the ridge. They used these oval structures for an activity that is believed to have combined sport with religious enactment. Many other ballcourts have been found in Hohokam sites in the region.

The inhabitants of the Romero village developed a large agricultural field system that extends for more than half a mile from the southern end of the ridge toward the mountains. Archaeologists found the remains of cobble masonry field houses, rock piles, and rock terrace borders. Vegetables and grains grown here would have been supplemented by wild plant foods gathered throughout the area.

In 1949, a hunter hiking through the Santa Catalina foothills four miles from the Romero Ruin made a remarkable discovery: a ceramic jar filled with a hundred thousand used stone and shell beads and about thirty copper bells. It would have taken about twenty-five thousand work hours just to make the beads, and the bells were probably traded from far to the south! One wonders who made these items and why such a treasure trove was buried in this way.

To see the Romero Ruin, park across the main road and follow an easy loop trail that is just under half a mile long and takes about half an hour. Interpretive signs are strategically situated along the way. In addition to the remains of the Hohokam village, you will see the ruins of an historic ranch house that belonged to Francisco and Victoriana Romero in the late 1800s. The Romeros constructed their residence and outbuildings right on top of the Hohokam site, probably recycling some of the ancient building stones for their own use.

As has been the case at so many ancient sites in the Southwest, folk legends developed regarding the origins of this site. Some believed the Romero ranch compound to be the remains of a long lost Spanish mission, the Mission of Ciru, and yes, they thought a trove of buried treasure had only to be dug up. Enticed by such stories, looters fruitlessly dug holes in the floors of the Romero compound, thus compromising historical information that would otherwise have been available to later researchers.

Catalina State Park is but a short drive from Tucson, where travel facilities can be found in abundance. While in the area, you will be rewarded by a visit to the Arizona State Museum at the University of Arizona. It has permanent and changing exhibits about the Indian cultures of southern Arizona.

Suggested reading: *Archaeology in the Mountain Shadows: Exploring the Romero Ruin*, by Deborah L. Swartz and William H. Doelle, Center for Desert Archaeology, Tucson, 1996.

# The Hardy Site

*The Hardy Site is located in Fort Lowell Park at 2900 North Craycroft Road in the northeast part of Tucson, Arizona. Information: (520) 885-3832.*

First reported in 1884 by the archaeological explorer, Adolph F. Bandelier, the Hardy Site contains the remains of a Hohokam village that once covered about a quarter of a square mile. Hohokam Indians lived here from about A.D. 300 to 1250. After they left, their homes disintegrated and melted into the ground. In 1873, the United States army built Fort Lowell directly over this ancient Indian site. Adobe bricks made to construct the fort's buildings contain potsherds and chips of worked stone.

After Fort Lowell was abandoned in 1891, the Hohokam site beneath it was disturbed by the construction of Tucson houses and apartments. In 1975, when Fort Lowell park was being developed, an onlooker noticed artifacts in the construction site. His observation led to archaeological excavations of a small portion of the site by the Arizona State Museum in the late 1970s.

The archaeologists uncovered clusters of pithouses, trash mounds, outdoor roasting pits, caliche mining pits, work areas, and a cemetery and offertory plaza. After completing their work, they backfilled the excavations to preserve them. Except for a trash mound, there are no ruins to be viewed.

The Hohokam of the Tucson Basin were related culturally to other Hohokam people farther north along the Gila and Salt rivers. They were attracted to the Tucson Basin by its abundant natural resources and long growing season. The basin is enclosed by five discontinuous mountain ranges from whose slopes sediments eroded to collect in the valley. Along the valley floor flow streams that the Indians used for floodwater farming. Rather than create an extensive irrigation canal network, as did the Hohokam of the Phoenix Basin, the Hardy folk directed flooding stream waters to their croplands, which were situated close to the water courses. This technique was especially effective in the rainy seasons of late winter and midsummer. Historical reports indicate that these streams used to flow year-round and were marked by beaver dams and cottonwoods and mesquite groves. Today, water in southern Arizona is too precious a commodity to be allowed to flow down river beds.

As the Hohokam established themselves in the Tucson Basin, agriculture evolved to be the mainstay of their economy. The Hardy residents took advantage of the fertile bottomlands southwest of the confluence of Pantano Wash and Rillito Creek to raise corn, beans, squash, and cotton. They also let wild edible plants such as pigweed, sunflower, and tansy mustard grow along the borders of their fields. They traded cotton and cotton products with their neighbors to the north.

The Hohokam also collected a wide variety of desert plants, seeds, and fruits to eat or use in other ways. Many plants that we think of as useless weeds served a purpose to ancient Indians. Readers interested in this aspect of Hohokam life will enjoy Gary Nabhan's book, *Gathering the Desert* (University of Arizona Press, 1987).

Apart from the effects of urban development, one reason that so little remains of the Hardy Site is that most houses were single story and built of sticks and mud. Over time, the wood decomposed and the mud walls reverted to desert soil. The City of Tucson sponsored archaeological research here, reconstructed a pithouse floor out of cement, put up a series of panels illustrating Hohokam life and culture, and created a display of artifacts in the Fort Lowell Museum. To learn more about the Hohokam of this area, visits to the Romero Ruin (p. 45) and the Arizona State Museum on the University of Arizona campus are suggested.

Suggested reading: *Hohokam Indians of the Tucson Basin,* by Linda M. Gregonis and Karl J. Reinhard, The University of Arizona Press, Tucson, Arizona, 1979.

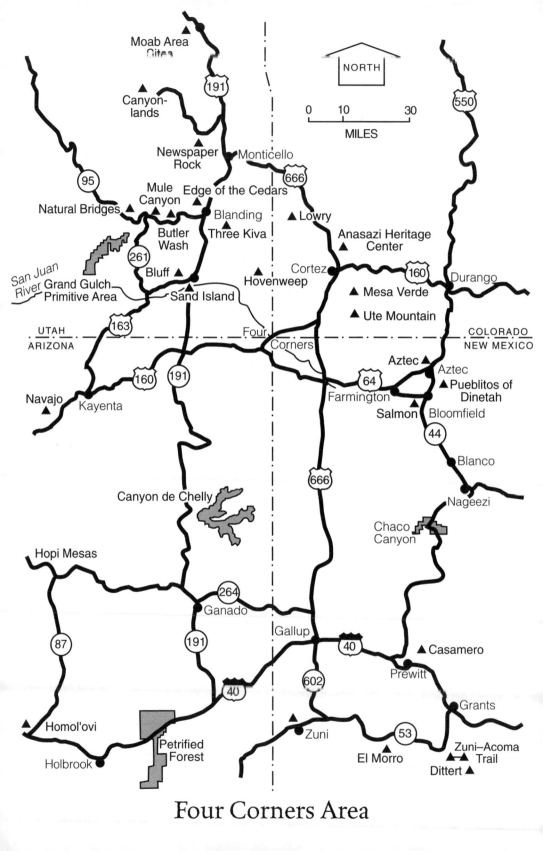

# Four Corners Area

# The Anasazi
## Ancestors of the Pueblo Indians

B est known among the prehistoric peoples of the American Southwest are the Anasazi, or Pueblo ancestors. This culture emerged more than two millennia ago from a seminomadic hunter-gatherer tradition to practice agriculture and live in villages. First sheltering themselves from the harsh winters of the Colorado Plateau in crude, shallow pithouses under rock overhangs, the Anasazi later acquired architectural skills with which they built multistoried masonry pueblos. It is these sites that form the major part of the present guidebook.

Anasazi is the word Navajos gave archaeologists, referring to the former inhabitants of abandoned cliff dwellings and pueblos. It stuck. The term "Pueblo ancestors" also sometimes is used, and the Hopi use a word in their own language, Hisatsinom. Despite frequent romantic but misleading inferences in popular literature, the ruins found in the Four Corners region represent neither a vanished race nor a lost civilization. As one Pueblo historian once commented to his largely non-Indian audience, "After visiting the ruins of the Parthenon, do you conclude that the Greeks mysteriously disappeared?"

The Anasazi–Pueblo people are alive and well, still living in Arizona and New Mexico. While their culture is much changed since the heyday of Cliff Palace or Pecos Pueblo, a cultural continuum can be traced from one period to the next over two thousand years. The story is told in legend and has been documented by archaeologists. When you visit sites described in this book, then go to a Pueblo feast day, you yourself will be able to attest to the vitality of Anasazi–Pueblo culture, past and present.

*Prehistoric Pueblo pictographs, Canyon de Chelly.*

From about 5,500 B.C. to A.D. 500, small scattered bands or family groups roamed the Southwest as they hunted small game and collected edible plants, seeds, nuts, and fruit. Over many centuries, these hunter-gatherers, whom we name the Archaic or Desert culture, acquired a growing knowledge of and interest in how to control the plants they used. When they acquired the all-important domestic grain, maize or corn, which had long been preeminent in southern Mexico, they began to shift away from nomadism. This transition to agriculture was the genesis of the Anasazi culture.

Because of the many finely woven baskets found at their pithouse sites, archaeologists refer to the first Anasazi as Basketmakers. By A.D. 700, these early farmers were building above-ground attached masonry dwellings, or pueblos. Then, the term Basketmaker is dropped in favor of Pueblo. As noted in the chart on page 54, Pueblo culture is divided into five time periods, numbered I to V. These categories are commonly used in archaeological literature and museum exhibits.

Through the centuries, the Anasazi improved their farming methods, invented more specialized tools and utensils, exalted their architecture, and developed beautiful craft arts and a complex religion. As their numbers grew, their territory expanded until theirs was the dominant culture from south-central Utah to east of the Rio Grande and from southern Colorado to southern New Mexico. Anasazi traders traveled to the Gulf of California, the Great Plains, and deep into Mexico.

While archaeologists note many groupings within the Anasazi–Pueblo culture, three main ones stand out: the Chacoan (centered in Chaco Canyon, New Mexico); the Mesa Verdean or Northern San Juan (centered around present-day Cortez, Colorado); and the Kayenta (centered around Kayenta, Arizona). Anasazi culture flourished in the Four Corners region in the twelfth and early thirteenth centuries. Then something happened, and by A.D. 1300, they had left.

Researchers have proposed a number of abandonment and migration theories, most of which probably contain elements of truth. And Pueblo Indians have stories and myths about this period of the past. We know that a severe drought struck the Four Corners region between A.D. 1275 and 1299, probably causing malnutrition. This, in turn, may have led to disease, an increased death rate and lowered birth rate, civil strife, and even rebellion against religious leaders. Other factors may have kicked in, too, such as soil erosion and depletion of natural resources, including game and fuel wood. People sought new places to live.

What perplexes scholars is that the regions abandoned were never reoccupied. Deserted pueblos and cliff dwellings were left undisturbed until European-Americans settled the old Anasazi country in the nineteenth century.

One part of the Anasazi–Pueblo world that thrived after the Four Corners exodus was the Rio Grande Valley. The pueblos and cave dwellings of Bandelier National Monument (p. 196), for example, were built at this time and many existing communities grew in size. Other areas populated by Four Corners folk were the Hopi region, the Little Colorado River, and the Zuni Mountains. In the mid-1500s, the first European explorers to arrive in the Southwest encountered this widespread and vigorous Pueblo culture.

*Black-on-white mug,*
*Edge of the Cedars museum.*

Spanish settlement of New Mexico marks a new era in Anasazi–Pueblo history. In the 1600s, Pueblo Indians experienced an invasion of Spanish soldiers, settlers, and Franciscan priests who introduced awesome new war technology, diseases to which they had no natural immunity, a foreign religion, and an oppressive civil authority. The native population began to decline and cultural changes came about as never before. The Spanish introduced metal tools, new seeds to plant, and domestic animals such as sheep, horses, and cattle. They also

| ANASAZI CHRONOLOGY | | | |
|---|---|---|---|
| Date | Pecos Classification | Robert's Classification | Characteristics and Events |
| 200 B.C.–A.D. 450 | Basketmaker I Basketmaker II | Basketmaker | Hunters and gatherers turning to horticulture. Habitations in caves. Atlatl in use. No pottery. Basketry. |
| 450–700 | Basketmaker III | Modified Basketmaker | Pithouse villages. Pottery made. Bow and arrow in use. |
| 700–900 900–1100 | Pueblo I Pueblo II | Developmental Pueblo | Above-ground pueblos. Pithouse becomes kiva. Cotton in use. |
| 1100–1300 | Pueblo III | Great Pueblo | Population expansion in up-lands. Advances in agricul-ture, architecture, crafts. Developed complex socio-religious organization. Cliff dwellings. |
| 1300–1700 | Pueblo IV | Regressive Pueblo | Resettlement in new areas. Social and economic change. |
| 1700–present | Pueblo V | Historic Pueblo | Strong influence from European culture. Much social, cultural, economic change. Some traditions continue. |

concentrated Pueblo populations around Franciscan missions, demand-ed tribute in the form of food, clothing, and labor, and suppressed native religious practices. In 1680, the Pueblos rose up in a successful revolt, which led to twelve years of independence before once again being overwhelmed by Spanish might.

The culture of the Pueblos became a mix of ancestral traditions and customs introduced by Europeans. Their religion, for example, survived despite long repression, but came to be practiced side by side, as it were, with Christianity. Tiwa, Tewa, and other Pueblo languages con-tinued, but many Indians learned Spanish and later English. One important continuity was land; grants bestowed by Spain were later honored by Mexico and the United States.

The descendants of the Anasazi, then, have integrated two worlds; a computer programmer in Los Alamos may devote many off-hours to practicing religious rituals that have survived from ancient roots. The

*Modern-day Pueblo dancers in New Mexico.*

following chapters are concerned not just with dusty old ruins, but also with the history of a living people whom we can meet, whether we are traveling or living in the Southwest. A better understanding of the past will give us a deeper appreciation of the present Southwest in all its fascinating dimensions.

> Suggested reading: *The Anasazi,* by J. J. Brody, Rizzoli, New York, New York, 1990 and *The People,* by Stephen Trimble, School of American Research Press, Santa Fe, New Mexico, 1993.

## Mesa Verde National Park

*The entrance to Mesa Verde National Park is along U.S. 160 midway between Cortez and Mancos in southwestern Colorado. It is a 15-mile drive from the park entrance to the visitor center and another 6 miles to the museum on Chapin Mesa. Information: (970) 529-4465. Entrance fee.*

For more than a century, the ruins of Mesa Verde have inspired visitors from across America and around the world. "A little city of stone asleep...still as sculpture...looking down into the canyon with the calmness of eternity," Willa Cather wrote of one cliff dwelling. More recently and less romantically, others have referred to Mesa Verde as the Disneyland of American archaeology. In truth, the cliff houses set in rock alcoves or tucked in cracks in the canyon walls do give a feeling of fantasy; sometimes they seem more the invention of a Hollywood set designer than the remnants of ancient communities.

To the Wetherills, the Mancos ranching family who discovered and explored many Mesa Verde cliff dwellings in the late nineteenth century—sites long known to local Ute Indians—the mesa was a rough, remote area suited only to grazing cattle. But today that wild mesa is tamed. Streams of summer tourists park their cars at the scenic overlooks, troop behind guides along paved walkways, and enjoy the amenities of a modern resort. From an almost forbidding wilderness of underbrush and labyrinthine canyons that made passage all but impossible, Mesa Verde has become the most popular archaeological preserve in North America.

Richard Wetherill's successful collecting of artifacts on Mesa Verde, assisted in 1891 by the young scientifically trained Swedish visitor, Gustav Nordenskiold, led him to give up ranching in favor of searching for and investigating ancient ruins in many other areas of the Four Corners region. He and his brothers and friends made spectacular discoveries and were disappointed only by the apathetic response of academics of the day: Native American antiquities then did not have the status of Old World archaeology. Were Richard Wetherill alive today, he would no doubt be astonished by the intense fascination of modern generations in his beloved cliff dwellings.

Although hunter-gatherers certainly roamed these canyons for thousands of years, Mesa Verde was not permanently settled until around A.D. 600. At this time, numerous pithouse villages were home to extended families. These Basketmaker sites date considerably later than similar ones in the lowlands surrounding the mesa; apparently it took early Puebloan farmers some time to learn the advantages of living in this high country.

Why did people choose to live here? The mesa offered good soils, timber for house construction, plenty of wood for fuel, and extra precipitation compared to lower elevations. Other advantages included springs, game, nutritious and medicinal native plants, and quarries for obtaining the materials needed to make tools and utensils.

Although pithouses are snug and secure, the Mesa Verdeans may have yearned to live above ground. By A.D. 750, they had begun building surface rooms of wattle and daub—upright posts woven through with slender branches to form walls that were then coated with mud. While these were airy, comfortable shelters in summer, they afforded inadequate protection from the sharp winds and deep snows of Colorado winters. Perhaps for this reason, small contiguous masonry rooms eventually took their place as living quarters. The people continued to build pithouses, however, now using them for community gatherings and for ceremonial purposes rather than as residences.

In popular belief, all Mesa Verdeans were cliff dwellers, but in fact, most lived in pueblos on top of the mesas. An example is Far View House, which was first settled in A.D. 900 and by 1100 housed some five hundred people. This site is along the road and open to the public.

*Cliff Palace, the largest cliff dwelling in the Southwest.*

It was not until around A.D. 1200 that many people moved into the canyons to live in the cliff dwellings. Their building sites were the south facing vaulted shallow caves and rock overhangs. By the mid-1200s, these cliff dwellings housed about half the population of Chapin Mesa. The new villages were somewhat isolated from each other, but their occupants would have met frequently along the trails to springs, on hunting and gathering forays, and occasionally at ceremonies at Sun Temple and Fire Temple, which you also can visit. The Mesa Verdeans lived in their cliff dwelling—Spruce Tree House, Cliff Palace, Balcony House, Long House, Mug House, and others—relatively briefly. By A.D. 1300, these pueblos were vacant.

Cliff dwellings and other contemporaneous sites often have defensive attributes, but evidence of warfare is scarce, and an old theory that the Anasazi were driven away by invaders from the north is not substantiated in the archaeological record. Affected by an extended drought and shortages of food and firewood, people trickled away.

*Classic black-on-white kiva jar. Chapin Mesa Museum, Mesa Verde.*

In recent decades, new archaeological research in southwestern Colorado has thrown a fresh perspective on Mesa Verde's place in the region. Investigations at the remains of eight large Anasazi towns in the Montezuma Valley near Cortez have revealed a prehistoric population dwarfing that of Mesa Verde. The population of Yellow Jacket alone may have equaled that of Mesa Verde at its peak. These towns, most of which now are held in trust by the Archaeological Conservancy and the Bureau of Land Management, hold much promise for future research.

Archaeological studies on Mesa Verde began in 1908 when Edgar Lee Hewett, author of the nation's first Antiquities Act, turned Harvard student Alfred Vincent Kidder loose on the mesa to map all the major cliff dwellings. Accompanying him with a camera was 20-year old Jesse Nusbaum, who years later was appointed park superintendent. Using creative initiatives in an era less hindered by federal bureaucracy and regulation, Nusbaum stabilized many sites and obtained funding to build the stone-and-timber headquarters, museum, and staff residences.

Between 1908 and 1922, the experienced archaeologist Jesse Walter Fewkes conducted excavations at Spruce Tree House, Cliff Palace, Sun Temple, Far View Ruin, and Pipe Shrine House. Another individual who devoted a large portion of his career to Mesa Verde archaeology was James A. Lancaster, a local farmer who learned the archaeologist's trade through years of on-the-job experience. In more recent years, contributors to the substantial body of archaeological information on Mesa Verde have included Douglas Osborne, Arthur H. Rohn, and Alden C. Hayes, to name a few. The results of their collected works fill a large bookcase.

Access to Mesa Verde National Park's cliff dwellings on Chapin and Wetherill mesas varies according to the season, and reservations for

*Square Tower House at Mesa Verde.*

guided tours are required to visit certain cliff dwellings. A visitor's first stop, therefore, should be the Far View Visitor Center, fifteen miles into the park, where tour information is available. In summer, many sites are open to visitors either by self-guided or ranger-guided tours; off-season, the selection is limited.

You can also follow the twelve-mile Ruins Road, which includes two driving loops that pass a series of mesa-top pithouses and pueblo ruins, as well as cliff-house overlooks. From the Cliff Palace trailhead, you can look down on this two hundred-room cliff dwelling, the largest in the Southwest. Balcony House, when it is open, offers an interesting and adventuresome hiking experience. Half a day will allow you a glimpse of the park: a couple of sites and the fine museum on Chapin Mesa. For a more complete experience, plan to spend a full day or longer.

In summer, the park schedules talks at sites, campfire talks at Morefield Campground, and nature walks for children. Far View Lodge is open from about May 1 to mid-October. Other conveniences include a gas station, general store, self-service laundry, and snack bar. More travel services are available in Cortez, Mancos, and Durango.

Mesa Verde is a true natural and archaeological wonder. Remember, however, that while more sites are open in summer, you will be contending with large numbers of visitors. To see the park in a quieter atmosphere, visit it off-season or consider taking a tour of the sites in Ute Mountain Tribal Park.

Suggested reading: *Understanding the Anasazi of Mesa Verde and Hovenweep*, edited by David Grant Noble, Ancient City Press, Santa Fe, New Mexico, 1992.

# Ute Mountain Tribal Park

*Ute Mountain Tribal Park is in the Mesa Verde–Mancos Canyon area outside the boundaries of the national park. Guided tours depart from the Visitor Center Museum, at the junction of Highways 160 and 666, 20 miles south of Cortez, Colorado. Information and reservations: (800) 847-5485 or (970) 749-1448. Entrance fee.*

Between early April and the end of October, the Ute Mountain tribe conducts half-day, full-day, and remote-country guided tours to archaeological sites within its 125,000-acre tribal park. Tours depart at 8:30 A.M.

When European-American settlers first came to southwestern Colorado, the region belonged to the Ute Indians. The descendants of one band of Utes live on a reservation south of Cortez. Their tribal park has been called "the other Mesa Verde" because it too contains a wealth of Anasazi cliff dwellings and surface ruins, as well as Anasazi and Ute rock art sites. It is fitting that these archaeological resources are in the custody of Native Americans whose ancestors roamed this land many

*Eagle Nest, a fortress-like cliff dwelling in Ute Mountain Tribal Park.*

generations ago.

The Anasazi–Pueblo sites in the park share the same general history as those in Mesa Verde National Park and readers are referred to the preceding chapter for this information.

Visiting Ute Mountain Tribal Park is a special experience. Absent are the crowds, commercialism, and tourist amenities of the famous national park next door. Here you will see these pristine cliff dwellings in a more relaxed atmosphere with a Ute Indian guide. The half-day tour is limited to sites in the scenic lower Mancos River Canyon, whereas the full-day version includes hiking to several more remote cliff dwellings. In Lion Canyon, you will follow a one-and-a-half mile rustic cliffside trail to Tree House, Lion House, Morris V, and Eagle Nest. Along the way you can linger to enjoy canyon panoramas and take pictures, walk in and around rooms, pick up (and put down) artifacts, and converse with your guide. The hike does involve some climbing and use of ladders.

Mancos Canyon was first surveyed in 1874 by a small offshoot party of the famous Hayden Expedition, which explored the Rocky Mountains. After mapping the Yellowstone area and the Tetons, Ferdinand V. Hayden sent his photographer, William Henry Jackson, ahead with a small party. While outfitting in Denver, Jackson heard a tale about abandoned cliff houses in the rough canyon country of southwestern Colorado. His imagination piqued, he went on to investigate. One evening, after a long day's ride, he and his group were camped in lower Mancos Canyon, discouraged that their arduous travels had not yet confirmed the story. Then, one member looked up and spotted "something that appeared very much like a house." The following day, they climbed up to the site, and lugging his heavy view camera and glass plates, Jackson made the first photograph of a Mesa Verde cliff dwelling.

Along the Mancos Canyon road, you will pass several impressive rock art sites, including Ute pictographs showing human figures and horses with riders. One site is near the former dwelling of Chief Jack House, the last traditional chief of the Ute Mountain Tribe, who died in 1971 at the age of eighty-six. Since his death, the tribe has been governed by an elected chairman and council.

Following your guide, you can drive your own car on the tours, or for a nominal extra fee, ride in the van. The full-day tour involves about eighty miles of driving on dirt roads. Bring drinking water and food for the day. Special back-country tours also can be arranged. Call the park for reservations and current tour rates.

Cortez offers many travel services, or you can arrange to stay at a campground within the park. The tribe also manages an RV park at their casino along the highway. The many other archaeological parks in this Four Corners area can be the theme of a visit lasting several days.

Suggested reading: *Ute Mountain Tribal Park: The Other Mesa Verde,* by Jean Akens, Four Corners Publications, Moab, Utah, 1987. *People of the Shining Mountains,* by Charles S. Marsh, Pruett Publishing Company, Boulder, Colorado, 1982.

# Anasazi Heritage Center

*The Anasazi Heritage Center, 3 miles west of Dolores, Colorado, on Colorado 184, includes the Escalante and Dominguez ruins. The center is 18 miles north of the entrance to Mesa Verde National Park. Information: (970) 882-4811. Entrance fee.*

The Anasazi Heritage Center was an outgrowth of the largest archaeological research project ever carried out in the United States. This work began after 1968, when the federal government authorized the damming of the Dolores River and building of McPhee Reservoir. When federal lands are to be disturbed, an environmental impact study must be conducted to include mitigation of any archaeological resources, and in the Dolores valley, there were many. By the end of the project, archaeologists had found more than 1,600 sites, tested 120, and studied a wealth of scientific data.

The Escalante and the Dominguez ruins were excavated and stabilized to become part of the Center's interpretive program. The sites are

*Escalante Ruins near the Anasazi Heritage Center.*

named for two adventuring Franciscan fathers, who camped here in 1776 while attempting to find a trail from New Mexico to California. The Escalante Ruin was excavated with American Bicentennial funds on the two hundredth anniversary of their two thousand-mile trek.

The twenty-room Escalante pueblo sits on a hill above the Anasazi Heritage Center, overlooking the reservoir. To the south, the low ridge line of Mesa Verde lies darkly on the horizon. The pueblo was built around A.D. 1129 and occupied, except for two short periods of vacancy, until the early 1200s.

Certain architectural features, such as its large rectangular pre-planned roomblock that encloses a central kiva, and walls of dressed exterior stones with rubble and mud cores, indicate this "great house" was built by or under the direction of people from Chaco Canyon (p. 113). Its dominating hilltop position also is typically Chacoan. In contrast, the pottery found here is Mesa Verdean in style, a fact that gives some credence to an interesting hypothesis that the men here (the builders) were from Chaco Canyon and married local women (the potters). The two groups may well have spoken different languages. Even so, they made their lives together, shared responsibilities, and raised intertribal families.

The small Dominguez Ruin, next to the Center's parking area, is Mesa Verdean in style, not Chacoan, and probably housed a single family. In the course of excavating this site, archaeologists made a rare discovery: the remains of a thirty-five-year-old woman who had been buried with a large collection of artifacts and jewelry, including sixty-nine hundred beads. Since most archaeological evidence points to the Anasazi having had an egalitarian society, one wonders who this individual was.

The Dolores valley offered good areas for growing crops as well as for hunting deer, antelope, elk, and bighorn sheep. It also was along a trade route, linking its inhabitants with near and distant neighbors.

The Anasazi Heritage Center has an outstanding museum whose exhibits draw heavily on the material excavated during the Dolores Archaeological Program. Its "discovery area" has hands-on and interactive archaeological exhibits. You can grind corn on a metate, handle artifacts, and explore a CD-ROM program about Lowry Ruins (p. 70). In addition to its museum functions, the Center stores some two million artifacts and documents and supports a research laboratory, library, theater, and conference rooms.

You may wish to see the museum and browse the bookshop first and then take the fifteen-minute walk up to the Escalante Ruin. The towns of Dolores and Cortez have travel and tourist facilities, and you can camp and fish at the reservoir. Within a two-hour drive are at least four more major archaeological monuments.

Suggested reading: *The Archaeology and Stabilization of the Dominguez and Escalante Ruins,* Colorado State Office, Bureau of Land Management, Denver, Colorado, 1979.

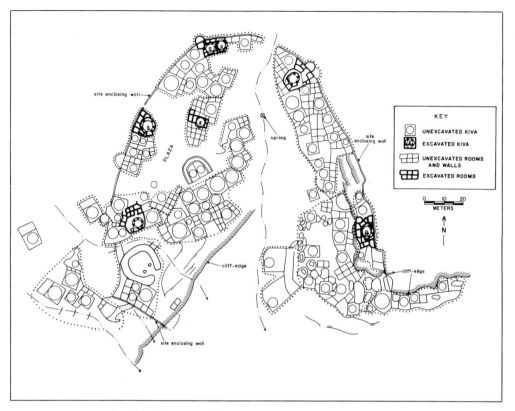

*Plan of Sand Canyon Pueblo. Courtesy Crow Canyon Archaeological Center.*

# Sand Canyon Pueblo

*Sand Canyon Pueblo is located northwest of Cortez, Colorado. From the intersection of U.S. 160 and 666 in Cortez, drive 4.8 miles north on 666, then turn west on County Road P, and continue 9.5 miles to the site. Information: (970) 247-4874.*

Sand Canyon Pueblo is one of a series of large prehistoric towns in the Montezuma Valley in the vicinity of Cortez, Colorado. The site was the subject of systematic archaeological investigations between 1983 and 1993, conducted by the Crow Canyon Archaeological Center in Cortez. Field work for this project was done by participants in Crow Canyon's educational programs under the direction of professional archaeologists. After excavation, the rooms were backfilled for better preservation. Thus, there is little to see at the site today in terms of features and standing architecture.

Sand Canyon is a horseshoe-shaped village surrounding a spring at the head of a canyon. This is part of the McElmo drainage, which flows into the San Juan River. From 1245 to 1290, the pueblo had a significant population, served as a ritual center, and was the focal point of many small settlements in the vicinity. Its estimated 725 residents lived in masonry dwellings around the edge of the canyon in what appears to have been a tightly knit community. The village consisted of 420 surface rooms, 90 kivas, 14 towers, an enclosed plaza, and other structures.

Excavations here have shown that this town was preplanned in design and built between the 1250s and 1270s. Its residents first built a massive stone wall that enclosed the houses and public buildings. The construction of this wall would have been a major community project, accomplished by people who did not as yet live here. Estimates are that a work force of thirty-six people would have taken about two months to do the job.

Sand Canyon is organized architecturally as a series of fourteen discrete roomblocks, each containing groups of residential and storage rooms associated with a kiva. While these rooms were part of the master plan, they were built and added to as needed.

The east side of this village appears to have been more residential in character than its west side. From their homes, the east-side residents would have had a good view across the canyon to the opposite side of the village with its more-public areas and structures. The west side, for example, had a community plaza, which was probably used for public events, such as dances, a large number of kivas, and a great kiva. The number of kivas at Sand Canyon indicates the degree to which these agriculturalists incorporated religion and ceremonialism into their lives and suggests that the village probably played an important role in the surrounding community.

Archaeological research at Sand Canyon addressed such specific questions as why the Anasazi of the Montezuma Valley left their many small dispersed pueblos to aggregate in towns, and if their apparent move toward social complexity and urbanization had something to do with their sudden abandonment of the region. While Sand Canyon was being excavated, other researchers associated with Crow Canyon surveyed the surrounding area and recorded more than five hundred sites. Still others conducted highly specialized archaeological and paleoenvironmental research. One scholar, for example, studied the use of turkeys, discovering that as the human population grew in the thirteenth century, the deer and rabbit populations decreased and domestic turkeys became an important source of meat protein.

Most of the published results of the Sand Canyon Project are in the form of technical reports with limited distribution; however, some information is available on-line at Crow Canyon's web site: www.crow-canyon.org. Here you will also find information on how to join Crow Canyon's public programs, which include archaeological digs and tours.

Sand Canyon Pueblo is controlled by the Bureau of Land Management's field office in Durango, Colorado. Although the ruins are backfilled, a trail with interpretive signs leads through the site. The town of Cortez has many travel services and is a convenient base from which to visit nearby archaeological areas.

Suggested reading: *The Sand Canyon Archaeological Project: A Progress Report,* edited by William D. Lipe, Crow Canyon Archaeological Center, Cortez, Colorado, 1992.

# Hovenweep National Monument

*Hovenweep National Monument straddles the Colorado-Utah border west of Cortez, Colorado. Monument headquarters are located next to Square Tower Group on the road between Pleasant View, Colorado, and Hatch Trading Post, Utah. Directions to the monument are well marked at intersections. Information: (970) 529-4465.*

The poetic resonance of the word Hovenweep, which means "deserted valley" in the Ute language, suggests the desolation of this region's mesas and canyons. Viewing this sageland today, which barely supports a few range cattle and some scattered Navajo homesteads, one wonders how it could have once sustained a vigorous population of Anasazi farmers.

This archaeological park actually consists of six groups of ruins, four in Colorado and two in Utah, situated at the heads of draws that drain into lower McElmo Creek and the San Juan River. You can easily walk from the visitor center to the sites in Square Tower Canyon. Other groups, including Horseshoe, Holly, Hackberry, Cajon, and Cutthroat Castle, can be reached by car, then hiking.

Hunter-gatherers lived in this region long before the Anasazi culture appeared around A.D. 500. At that time, the open flatlands offered deeper soils and better forage—overgrazing has destroyed the original grasses—than they do today, allowing the Anasazi to live here for hundreds of years. Around A.D. 1150, however, changes occurred and the inhabitants of the area began building larger pueblos around fortess-like stone towers at the heads of box canyons. In these locations, moisture percolated through the porous sandstone on the mesas to an impervious layer of shale and flowed laterally underground to emerge at the canyon heads in the form of seeps and springs. The Indians built check dams and reservoirs to better control this precious water supply as well as the occasional floodwaters that spilled over the canyon rims. This system allowed them to cultivate garden plots on the terraced slopes of the lower canyons and to encourage the growth of other native edible or useful plants, such as beeweed, ground cherry, sedges, milkweed, cattail, and wolf berry.

The Hovenweep people built massive stone structures encircling the canyon heads, often called "castles" by nineteenth-century explorers. And within the canyons, in some places just below the spring, they erected tall stone towers of varying configurations: square, oval, circular, or D-shaped. The masonry and engineering skills of the builders are evident. A few still-standing structures are perched on huge boulders of fallen rimrock. Except for some narrow peepholes, they are virtually windowless, and at least one has no door—it must have been entered by ladder from the rooftop.

The purpose and function of the towers remains an enigma. Were they forts, situated to guard the springs? Did they serve as lookouts, signal towers, or celestial observatories? Or did they have a ceremonial function that we can only guess at?

The Indians left their Hovenweep pueblos in the late 1200s and never returned. Their departure coincided with the Anasazis' abandonment of the entire Four Corners region and migration to other parts of the Southwest. The towers they left behind stand like enduring sentinels of their progression through time and space.

The first Europeans to see the Hovenweep ruins were members of an 1854 Mormon party. Six decades later, the archaeologist Jesse Walter Fewkes described them in his report, *Prehistoric Villages, Castles, and Towers of Southwestern Colorado,* published by the Smithsonian Institution. Since then, little formal archaeological work has been conducted at these sites, possibly due to their having been thoroughly looted over the years. In the 1970s, limited investigations were carried out by Joseph C. Winter and others of the Hovenweep Archaeological Project.

You should begin your tour of Hovenweep at the visitor center and the Square Tower complex of sites. This walk through the ruins takes an hour or more. From here you can obtain directions to other outlying sites. All ruins are fragile and should not be climbed on. A couple of cautionary notes: Most local roads are unpaved and become slippery when wet; and while few humans live in this region, many rattlesnakes do.

The monument maintains a campground near the visitor center. Drinking water is available, but you must bring your own food and firewood. Other travel services and accommodations can be found in Cortez, Bluff, and Blanding.

Suggested reading: *The Towers of Hovenweep,* by Ian Thompson, Mesa Verde Museum Association, Mesa Verde National Park, Colorado, 1993.

*Square Tower House at Hovenweep National Monument.*

# Lowry Ruins

*Lowry Ruins are near the town of Pleasant View along U.S. 666 in south-western Colorado. From Route 666 in Pleasant View, drive 9 miles west following road signs to the site. Information: (970) 882-4811.*

Today, as you drive through the rich farmlands between Pleasantville and Lowry Ruins, you will get a sense of the agricultural potential of the Montezuma Valley. Eight hundred years ago, when Lowry Pueblo was at its height, agriculture sustained an Anasazi community numbering in the thousands.

Lowry was one of eight major Anasazi towns that dotted the Montezuma Valley in the 1100s and 1200s. The largest, Yellow Jacket, by itself had a population of about 2,500. Another was Sand Canyon Pueblo (p. 65), which was recently partially excavated by the Crow Canyon Archaeological Center in Cortez. In those days, the valley's population was larger than it is today.

Scores of books have been written about Mesa Verde, after which this northern branch of the Anasazi culture was named, but only in recent years have researchers begun to appreciate the significance of the Montezuma Valley communities. What they now realize is that these towns were the real center of the northern Anasazi culture.

Lowry's centerpiece is its great house, which dates to the time when the Chaco phenomenon (p. 113) was at its peak, between around A.D. 1030 to 1140. It is the northernmost known Chacoan outlier. However we think of Chaco—as an ideology, a trade network, a military power, or a system incorporating all of the above—Lowry was way out on the frontier. It was a long trek from here to Chaco Canyon. Still, the great house has distinctive Chacoan features: an elevated building site, strong construction with fine core-and-veneer masonry, interior kivas and a nearby great kiva, and roads.

In the immediate vicinity of the Lowry great house, archaeologists have recorded more than a hundred other sites: small pueblos, field houses, shrines, storage structures, and a water-control system that included reservoirs. Only a small fraction of this large complex has been excavated. What is more, a dozen other communities existed within a six-mile radius of here.

The Lowry great house was constructed in phases between A.D. 1089 and 1120 and was inhabited until about 1150. Most of the building probably had two stories, but some sections may have been higher. Situated on a ridge, it was the dominant structure in the community. Another nearby pueblo was the Pigg Site, located just across the fence to the east. It was excavated in the 1990s by archaeology students from Fort Lewis College under the tutelage of W. James Judge, who directed the Chaco Project in the late 1970s and early 1980s.

*Lowry Pueblo, a Chacoan outlier.*

Chaco and its regional outlier system collapsed beginning around A.D. 1140, which is when the Lowry great house fell into disuse. But the community and others in the valley thrived until the late 1200s. What brought about the end of the Chacoan period, and what caused Anasazi life in this region to end, form two of the major current questions in the field of American archaeology.

Lowry Ruins were missed by the Dominguez–Escalante Expedition of 1776 and missed again by the Hayden Expedition of 1881. Subsequent settlers gave the site little notice, and it was not recorded until 1919, when it was named for George Lowry, an early homesteader. It was excavated in the early 1930s by Paul S. Martin of the Chicago Field Museum of Natural History. Today the site is administered by the Bureau of Land Management.

There are picnic tables near the site, and brochures are available to guide you along the ruins trail. A CD-ROM, *People in the Past: The Ancient Puebloan Farmers of Southwest Colorado*, is available for sale at the Anasazi Heritage Center in Dolores (p. 62); it has good information on the prehistory of Lowry and Anasazi–Pueblo culture. A visit to nearby Hovenweep National Monument with its towers should also be made. Travel services are available in Cortez and Monticello.

Suggested reading: *Yellow Jacket: A Four Corners Anasazi Ceremonial Center*, by Frederick Lange, et al., Johnson Books, Boulder, Colorado, 1986.

# Three Kiva Pueblo

*Three Kiva Pueblo is located in Montezuma Canyon in southeastern Utah. The site is along Montezuma Canyon Road about 15 miles north of Hatch Trading Post and 23 miles south of the road's intersection with U.S. 163, south of Monticello. Information: (435) 587-2141.*

Three Kiva Pueblo, a fourteen-room Anasazi site, is an out-of-the-way Indian ruin that will be of more interest to archaeology buffs than to someone new at the game. Montezuma Canyon is an arid, unpopulated stretch of country whose scenic charm lies in contrasts between spare, rugged mesas and cottonwood-shaded dry washes. Much of this territory belongs to the Ute and Navajo tribes, the successors to the Anasazi Indians who lived here seven hundred to a thousand years ago.

William Henry Jackson, the noted American photographer and explorer, made the first archaeological reconnaissance of Montezuma Canyon in 1886. Excavations on nearby Alkali Ridge were carried out in 1908 and again in the 1930s. Three Kiva Pueblo itself was excavated between 1969 and 1972 by the Brigham Young University Field School of Archaeology.

*Three Kiva Pueblo.*

The very first section of the site was built in the ninth century. The pueblo subsequently experienced three occupations and building phases, with its main occupation between A.D. 1000 and 1300. Its earliest occupants were of the Kayenta branch of the Anasazi, whose central territory lay some distance to the south. But later, the Three Kiva people maintained closer ties with their Mesa Verde and Hovenweep neighbors to the east.

The pueblo was laid out as a square. Windblown fill on a kiva floor under the collapsed roof measured over two feet deep—a clue that the kiva survived intact for a long time after the villagers left. Just south of the pueblo is an interesting two-by-twenty foot masonry room identified as a turkey run from the abundance of turkey bones. Domesticated turkeys were an important source of food to the Anasazi, not just here but at many other sites. The Indians also wove blankets of turkey feathers and made whistles from the birds' leg bones.

In the course of the site's excavations, diggers found two abalone shell pendants, evidence that a trade network existed to the Pacific Coast. Predictably, they also found many stone tools: knives, scrapers, drills, spear and arrow points, hammer stones, hoes, axes, mauls, and grinding stones. Artifacts such as these helped archaeologists reconstruct a picture of daily life at the pueblo hundreds of years ago.

The Bureau of Land Management curates this site and restored one of its kivas, which you may enter by ladder. If you hike down the canyon a short distance from the site, you will find Ute petroglyphs along the east-facing walls, including buffaloes, cranes, and abstract figures.

The road to this site is unpaved and crisscrosses the wash numerous times. Be careful of flash flooding and getting stuck in dry sand. Gas, restaurants, and overnight accommodations can be found in Bluff, Blanding, and Monticello.

Suggested reading: "A Syntheses of Excavations at Site 42SA863, Three Kiva Pueblo, Montezuma Canyon, San Juan County, Utah," by Donald E. Miller, 1974, unpublished Master's thesis available from Brigham Young University, Provo, Utah.

# Edge of the Cedars State Park

*Edge of the Cedars State Park is in the southeastern Utah town of Blanding on U.S. 163 between Bluff and Monticello. Directions to the park are clearly marked in town. Information: (435) 678-2238.*

Edge of the Cedars Pueblo once thrived on the northern periphery of Anasazi territory. Situated on a ridge overlooking Westwater Canyon, it had a panoramic view over the surrounding countryside. To the north lie the Abajo Mountains, a rich area for hunting and foraging, and to the southeast you can see Shiprock, a famous geologic landmark. In earlier times, this well-watered region produced sufficient agricultural products to support a high-density population. Old timers in Blanding have reported seeing the remnants of irrigation ditches and check dams around Edge of the Cedars Pueblo.

Anasazi Indians, the ancestors of modern Pueblo Indians, lived here between A.D. 850 and 950, again between 1025 and 1125, and possibly briefly again in the thirteenth century. At its peak, their pueblo consisted of six residential complexes, including ten kivas and one great kiva. One kiva was excavated and restored and may be entered by means of a ladder, which descends through a hatchway in the roof. A small roomblock has been restored, too, but the great kiva, which probably served as a community center, remains unexcavated and appears as a large shallow basin in the ground. The original village probably extended beyond its present park boundaries before early settlers cultivated the land to grow crops, in the process obliterating archaeological traces.

Weber State College field school excavated about 25 percent of this

*Edge of the Cedars Pueblo.*

site between 1969 and 1972. Unfortunately, because of lax student supervision, the archaeological documentation was poor, field notes and photographs were lost, and no final report ever was produced. One interesting find, however, was a prehistoric copper bell, a clue to prehistoric trading contacts between this region and the high cultures of Mexico, far to the south.

Edge of the Cedars Museum, which is open daily, contains exhibits relating to the peoples and cultures of southeastern Utah. These include the Anasazi, Navajo, and Ute Indians and Euro-American settlers. The museum has an outstanding collection of prehistoric ceramics and other artifacts and a mural reproducing some of the region's major pictographs. A trail guide is available to help you understand the site as you walk around.

Blanding is a small, quiet town with several cafes, gas stations, and motels. From Blanding, you might consider driving to Bluff to see the Sand Island Petroglyph Site (p. 93) or to take an archaeological rafting excursion on the San Juan River (p. 91).

# Canyonlands National Park

*Canyonlands National Park is in southeastern Utah. It can be accessed from Utah 211, north of Monticello, and Utah 313, north of Moab. The only other accesses are by unpaved roads and jeep trails. Information: (435) 259-7164. Entrance fee.*

Like Grand Canyon, Canyonlands is an extensive area that was set aside by Congress to preserve its extraordinary scenery and geologic formations sculpted by eons of erosion. By car, foot, horseback, or jeep, you can explore many strange landforms, from pinnacles and spires to fossil sand dunes, red rock cliffs, and precipitous canyons. Within the park, the waters of the Green River join those of the Colorado, soon to plunge through Cataract Canyon and flow into Lake Powell.

But Canyonlands was also once the home of prehistoric Native Americans who left their mark in the form of small scattered pueblos, snug granaries, and several outstanding pictograph galleries. Although relatively little archaeological work has been done in Canyonlands, the remains of several prehistoric groups have been recorded.

Thousands of years ago, hunter-gatherers roamed these canyons to gather wild edible plants and to mine minerals. While here, they painted large pictures of anthropomorphic beings on the cliff walls. These tall, ghost-like figures are believed to date to the late-Archaic period, between fifteen hundred and three thousand years ago.

The artists, probably shamans, used a variety of techniques to achieve special effects. In some cases, they smoothed the cliff surface, then applied paint directly with their fingers or yucca-fiber brushes, or blew pigments through reed tubes. They also incised lines through painted areas to create texture. Many of the pigments used are dark rusty red (from ground hematite). Some elements are faded, while others are decorated with white lines and dots. Examples of these Archaic pictographs in the Barrier Canyon style can be found in the backcountry on the west side of the park. The Great Gallery in Horseshoe Canyon and the Bird Site in the Maze District are especially noteworthy; however, one must backpack into these areas.

Anasazi farmers also lived in Canyonlands, patricularly between A.D. 950 and 1250. Like their Archaic antecedents, these Puebloan people hunted game and foraged for plant foods, but they also cultivated corn, beans, and squash in the region's sparse agricultural areas. Their settlements are found near the canyons' rare springs and intermittently flowing creeks. When drought struck the Four Corners region in the thirteenth century, these farmers left never to come back.

*Canyonlands from the Maze Overlook.*

*Pictographs, Barrier Canyon, Canyonlands National Park.*

In the Needles District on the east side of the river, the Roadside Ruin, a well-preserved Anasazi granary just west of the visitor center, is very accessible. Canyonlands has long been considered a frontier zone between the Fremont and Anasazi cultures, and no one is quite certain which group was responsible for some of the rock art. Some examples, including the much-photographed All American Man pictograph, can be reached by jeep in Salt Canyon and Ruin Park.

Overnight backcountry trips in Canyonlands require permits, which should be obtained by advance reservation. Whether you are hiking or jeeping into remote areas, please be sure that everyone in your party treats the archaeological sites with respect. Defacing them is a federal offense (p. 227), and even touching them can further their deterioration. Any observed problems should be reported to park officials. Traveling in the desert also can be hazardous to your health if you are not well prepared. This means bringing water and food, having driving experience on jeep trails, and knowing how to change a flat.

Green River and Monticello have travel services, and Moab is a major travel and tourist center where you can sign up for raft, jeep, and bicycle tours.

> Suggested reading: *Cultural Resource Inventory and Testing in the Salt Creek Pocket and Devils Lane Areas, Needles District, Canyonlands National Park,* by Betsy L. Tipps and Nancy J. Hewett, National Park Service, Denver, Colorado, 1989.

# Butler Wash Ruins

*Butler Wash Ruins are in southeastern Utah along Utah 95, 10.7 miles west of its intersection with Utah 191. The turnoff is clearly marked along the highway. A 1-mile loop trail leads from the parking area to the ruins overlook. Information: (435) 587-1532.*

Travelers along Utah 95 should take a driving break to see this picturesque cliff dwelling at the head of Butler Wash. From the highway rest area, a fifteen-minute walk will take you across the slickrock to a point where you can view the ruin.

This thirteenth-century cliff house consists of living and storage rooms and four kivas. It rests on a ledge in a cave within the cliff. A second alcove beneath it would have prohibited any assault by attackers. The site's only access was by means of a hand-and-toehold trail chipped into the rock face to the left of the caves. From the overlook you can still see this trail; however, erosion has worn away some of the steps. This cliff dwelling's defensibility is typical of Anasazi sites in the Four Corners region in the late 1200s. While little evidence of warfare has been found in the archaeological record, people must have felt very insecure during this time.

The Butler Wash cliff house is oriented to the south, which allowed the benefits of solar warming in winter, when the sun's rays penetrated deep within the cave. In the summer months, by contrast, the cliff's overhang provided shade to the inhabitants.

You will notice water stains flowing over the cliff edge directly above the pueblo, made by runoff from rains and snowmelt. This convenient drainage provided fresh water, even a natural plumbing system, to the cliff house occupants. Runoff also would have been channeled to down-canyon garden plots of corn, beans, and squash. Such products were stored in small masonry rooms tucked under rock ledges. One of these granaries is visible from the overlook to the left of the main cliff dwelling.

Along the trail to the overlook you will see numerous desert plants that were useful to the Indians. They harvested the fruit of the prickly

pear cactus, for example, and collected nuts of the piñon pine in the fall. These nuts are highly nutritious and will keep for years in good storage conditions. The Anasazi also used fibers from the yucca plant to make sandals, baskets, and rope, and they shredded cliffrose bark to fashion mats and other fabrics. Juniper berries, with which we flavor gin, were used as a food seasoning.

Butler Wash flows along the east side of Comb Ridge, a ninety-mile, east-sloping hogback along which many prehistoric Pueblo sites can be found. This geologic feature, through which the highway makes a dramatic cut just west of Butler Wash, was formed about seventy million years ago.

Other nearby ruins you may wish to see are at Mule Canyon (below), Grand Gulch (p. 82), and Natural Bridges National Monument (p. 85). Travel services are available in Blanding and Bluff.

## Mule Canyon Indian Ruins

*Mule Canyon Indian Ruins are located along Utah 95, 16 miles east of Natural Bridges National Monument and 20 miles west of the intersection of Utah 95 and U.S. 191. Information: (435) 587-1532.*

Mule Canyon Pueblo was inhabited in the eleventh and twelfth centuries when Anasazi Pueblo culture was at its height in the Four Corners region. The pueblo consists of an L-shaped masonry roomblock of twelve rooms, two kivas, and a two-story tower. The occupants used these rooms for living, for storing food and supplies, and as work areas in inclement weather. They carried on most of their daily activities, however, on the rooftops and in the plaza in front of the pueblo.

For a small site, Mule Canyon has several interesting features. One is the tower, which may have been used for signal communications with neighbors; a contemporaneous community with direct line of sight to Mule Canyon Pueblo lies only a mile to the east. Also curious are two tunnels leading from the kiva, one linking it to the tower, the other to the roomblock. Whether the tunnels had a practical or ceremonial function is open to question. People entered the kiva by way of a hatch in its roof. Other kiva features include a wall niche, a rectangular box, a fire pit, a ventilator shaft to draw in fresh air, a stone deflector to circulate the air, and pilasters to support roof beams.

This pueblo was first built around A.D. 750 and was fully occupied between 1000 and 1150. Artifacts found in the ruins indicate that the people had ties with both Mesa Verde and Kayenta Anasazi groups.

The University of Utah excavated this site. Later, the Bureau of Land Management developed it for Route 95 travelers to see. Construction of this highway, a major project funded by bicentennial grants, was not

*Butler Wash cliff dwelling.*

*Kiva at Mule Canyon Ruins showing tunnel entrance leading to tower.*

without controversy. Conflicts between pro- and anti development factions inspired Edward Abbey's popular novel, *The Monkey Wrench Gang.*

The surrounding area is Cedar Mesa, a large densely forested table-land cut by a series of canyons that had a significant pre-Columbian Indian population. Mormon pioneers on the famed Hole-in-the-Rock Expedition traversed Cedar Mesa in the winter of 1879–1880 to estab-lish southeastern Utah's first Euro-American settlement in Bluff.

Be sure to stop and see the Butler Wash Ruin (p. 79) and Natural Bridges National Monument (p. 85), both along Highway 95. You will find travel services in Blanding and Bluff, to the east, and Fry Canyon, to the west.

## Grand Gulch Primitive Area

*Grand Gulch is a tributary canyon of the San Juan River in southeastern Utah. Access is limited. For current information on obtaining a reservation and permit, contact the Bureau of Land Management, Monticello Field Office, P.O. Box 7, Monticello, Utah, 84535. Information: (435) 587-1532. Permit required.*

Grand Gulch is a sixty-mile-long canyon that meanders down through Cedar Mesa to join the San Juan River shortly before it enters the still waters of Lake Powell. Snowmelt, seasonal rains, and springs

*A protected pristine storage room in Grand Gulch.*

sustain lush undergrowth on the canyon floor, above which sandstone cliffs rise precipitously to the surrounding tableland.

Since Grand Gulch is accessible only to people traveling by foot or horseback, a visit here requires advance planning. However, this scenic and archaeologically fascinating canyon holds much reward to anyone with the time and ability to go there.

By A.D. 200 or so, the Cedar Mesa area, including Grand Gulch, was inhabited by the Colorado Plateau's earliest agriculturalists, known as the Basketmakers. Most of their inner-gulch sites are found under rock overhangs, sometimes beneath later Pueblo ruins.

The Basketmaker culture eventually was replaced by Puebloan farmers, who began living in the gulch sometime after A.D. 1000 and thrived there for three centuries. They built extended-family size cliff houses with storage granaries and farmed on the canyon bottom and up on Cedar Mesa. Some of their dwellings have survived in excellent condition with roofs intact and fingerprints still visible in the mud-plaster of the walls. You will enjoy the excitement of seeing artifacts such as potsherds, stone flakes, and dried corncobs. Please remember that the privilege of visiting well-preserved but fragile sites such as these involves an important responsibility: not to remove any artifacts, climb on walls, or touch the rock art.

Numerous amateur and professional archaeologists have worked in the Grand Gulch area over the past century, the first being Richard

*Pictograph panel in Grand Gulch.*

Wetherill, famed for his discovery of Mesa Verde's cliff dwellings. During his collecting expeditions here in the 1890s, he packed out large quantities of artifacts. This material remains in storage at New York City's American Museum of Natural History and Chicago's Field Museum.

Wetherill, who was a cattle rancher with little archaeological training, has been criticized for looting Grand Gulch's archaeological treasures; however, it must be said to his credit that when he excavated the pre-ceramic Basketmaker II sites here, he recognized that they represented a distinct culture antedating the overlying Pueblo remains. His theory of the existence of an early "basket people," which was later verified by trained archaeologists, was a breakthrough in the understanding of Southwestern prehistory.

You can obtain a brochure and hiking map from the BLM, and the staff at the Kane Gulch Ranger Station will help you locate major sites along the trail. You can enter Grand Gulch by way of Kane Gulch, Bullit Canyon, or Collins Spring. It is possible to do a day hike, or go on overnight or multiday trips. You can also enter by Kane Gulch (leaving your car at the ranger station), hike down the canyon, and exit by Bullit. A third option is to use a professional outfitter, who will pack in your food and gear and prepare your meals. Consult the BLM about these options.

Grand Gulch offers no amenities beyond what you carry with you. Ask about the availability of potable spring water in the canyon, but do not drink from the stream without a good filtration system. To enjoy

*Handprints on a cliff wall at Kachina Bridge.*

this experience you should be well prepared, in good physical condition, and alert to avoid accidents such as sprained ankles, snakebite, heat stroke, and dehydration. They can ruin the fun.

> Suggested reading: *Cowboys & Cave Dwellers: Basketmaker Archaeology in Utah's Grand Gulch,* by Fred M. Blackburn and Ray A. Williamson, School of American Research Press, Santa Fe, New Mexico, 1997.

## Natural Bridges National Monument

*Natural Bridges National Monument is located along Utah 95, 26 miles east of Fry Canyon and 42 miles west of Blanding, Utah. Information: (435) 692-1234. Entrance fee.*

In 1908, President Theodore Roosevelt set aside more than seven thousand acres around upper White Canyon in Utah to safeguard three outstanding geologic formations, or bridges. The park area, however, had long ago been a haven of the Anasazi Indians and contains several of their dwelling sites.

Since this canyon is in what used to be an extremely remote and rugged part of Utah, its natural bridges were not seen and recorded by white people until 1883, and not until 1961 did archaeologists formally survey this area. They found two hundred ancient sites. Many were small collapsed or buried structures on the juniper- or sage-covered mesa, but others were pueblos, granaries, and rock art within the canyon. In recent years, more extensive and thorough investigations have been conducted by the National Park Service.

While White Canyon's resources probably made it attractive to Archaic hunter-gatherers, its Pueblo occupation began around A.D. 450.

Then, in the mid-1100s the canyon saw an influx of people and a spurt of building. The inhabitants were Mesa Verde Anasazi who carried on active trade with inhabitants of the Kayenta Anasazi country to the south. Archaeologists have noted that a cultural lag existed between this northern peripheral region and communities in the Anasazi heartland along the San Juan River. This phenomenon is noticeable in pottery designs and building styles.

Tree-ring studies show that house construction around Natural Bridges ended in the 1250s, signalling a population decline. Around this same time, the Anasazi world as a whole began to experience major changes that ultimately resulted in a complete depopulation of the Four Corners region. For six hundred years, the vacant habitations of White Canyon remained undisturbed. Some cliff dwellings survived this long passage of time in excellent condition, even with roofs intact. Such preservation happens when an area is not later reoccupied by people who salvage building materials for their own uses.

When you visit Natural Bridges, take the scenic nine-mile driving loop to the bridge overlooks. Understandably, this park focuses its interpretive program on natural history; however, by consulting the ranger staff, you can learn about hiking trails leading past cliff dwellings and rock art sites. An unmaintained trail system (8.2 miles long) links all three bridges and loops back across the mesa to the starting point. From Horsecollar Ruin Overlook, you can take a trail to this interesting cliff dwelling. At Kachina Bridge, you will find several mud structures under a broad rock overhang on which a number of petroglyphs and pictographs are visible. Most of White Canyon's rock art dates to between A.D. 950 and 1300.

The Monument's visitor center includes exhibits and a slide program on the area's geology. You can camp here but the nearest places to purchase food, gas, and supplies are at Fry Canyon, Blanding, and Mexican Hat. Grand Gulch (p. 82) is only a few miles south on Highway 261, and Mule Canyon Ruins (p. 81) are about sixteen miles east on the way to Blanding.

Suggested reading: *An Archaeological Survey of the Upper White Canyon Area, Southeastern Utah,* by Philip M. and Audrey E. Hobler, Utah State Historical Society, Salt Lake City, Utah, 1978.

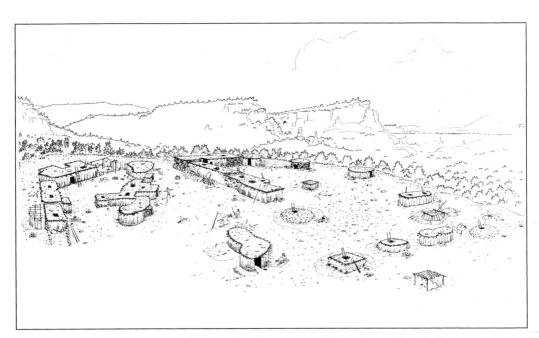

*Reconstruction of the Coombs Village, ca. A.D. 1100, at Anasazi State Park. Courtesy University of Utah Press. Drawing by George A. King.*

# Anasazi State Park

*Anasazi State Park is located in Boulder, a small town along Utah 12 in south-central Utah. Information: (435) 335-7308. Entrance fee.*

When Kayenta Anasazi people moved from what is now northeastern Arizona to the southern slopes of the Aquarius Plateau in the late 1000s, they had every reason to anticipate a prosperous existence. The area had fertile soils, reliable streams, plentiful game, abundant firewood, and raw materials for building houses and making pottery, tools, and clothing. Even the climate favored them: At an elevation of 6,700 feet, summers were pleasant and winters not too harsh. Compared with settlements in the Grand Canyon to the south, life at this Kayenta outpost was relatively comfortable.

The Coombs Site, which was excavated in the 1950s, is what remains of an ancient Indian settlement on the western border of the Anasazi world. Its former residents irrigated fields along local streams, hunted game ranging from bighorn sheep and mule deer to rodents and rabbits, and foraged for many edible wild plants and seeds. Archaeologists view the Coombs village as having been something of a cultural crossroads where Kayenta Anasazi settlers developed ties with their Fremont and Virgin River Anasazi neighbors.

The Coombs village thrived here for a little more than a century; then, around A.D. 1200, it was almost completely consumed by fire. What caused the conflagration is hard to determine today. Accidental fires probably were a common occurance in pueblos and were hard to put out once started. Many must have been caused when sparks from hearths ignited dry grass or twigs used as building materials in ceilings. The Coombs fire, however, may have been set intentionally. Although signs of violence do not appear in the recovered materials, archaeologists suspect foul play.

Another puzzle is where the Coombs people went after the disaster. As yet, no sites have been excavated that show a later occupation by these folk. Perhaps they broke up into small groups and returned south and east to join other Anasazi communities along the San Juan River. Their village, soon to be covered by dust and blowing dirt, lay undisturbed for more than seven centuries.

The visitor center includes a small museum displaying artifacts from the Coombs Site. From here, you exit to a pathway leading through the archaeological site. The first structure you will see is completely restored and offers a good idea how an Anasazi home originally looked. There is partially restored pithouse, too. The centerpiece of the site, however, is an L-shaped block of rooms, covered by a canopy, that has been left as it was when excavated. Interpretive signs explain various cultural and architectural features.

The excavations here were part of an extensive archaeological research project resulting from the building of Glen Canyon Dam. Although the waters of Lake Powell lie forty-five miles distant, research at this site, one of the largest prehistoric Pueblo ruins west of the Colorado River, was deemed essential to better understand the prehistory of the inundated region, which itself had few village sites.

You should allocate at least half an hour to tour the Coombs Site. Boulder has a restaurant, gas station, and general store. More travel services can be found in Escalante, the next town south on Utah 12. Anasazi State Park has a picnic area, and camping can be found at Calf Creek along Route 12 south of Escalante. The extraordinary scenic beauty of this region was officially recognized in 1998, when President Bill Clinton dedicated it as the Grand Staircase–Escalante National Monument. The area set aside includes almost two million acres of pristine wilderness marked by stunning geologic features.

Suggested reading: *The Coombs Site*, 3 vols., by Robert H. Lister, University of Utah Press, Salt Lake City, Utah, 1959–1961.

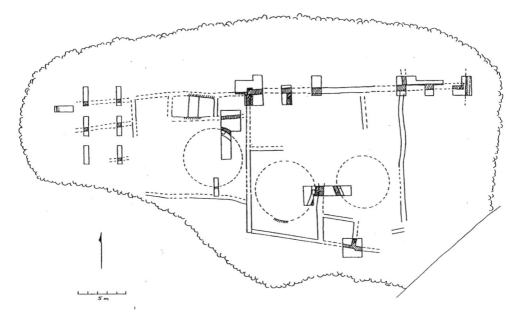

*Recent excavations at Bluff Great House began to reveal the site's layout. Sketch by Stephen H. Lekson.*

## Bluff Great House

*Bluff Great House is in the town of Bluff, in southeastern Utah. From downtown, take the cemetery road and you will pass the Bluff Great House site on the left.*

No aspect of the Southwest's prehistory more intrigues professional and avocational archaeologists than Chaco Canyon (p. 113) and the Chaco phenomenon. This phenomenon includes well over a hundred "great houses" dispersed over a wide region. These structures have architectural similarities to the much larger buildings for which Chaco Canyon is famed.

One great house is in the small resort town of Bluff, Utah, situated on the north bank of the San Juan River. In 1996, archaeologists Catherine M. Cameron and Stephen H. Lekson, along with several colleagues and students from the University of Colorado, began a long-term research project to investigate Bluff Great House. They are interested in finding out if and how this site was linked to Chaco Canyon and what its relationship was with sites in the immediate area. These questions are interesting to pose, but difficult to answer.

The great house is a tightly packed block of rooms overlooking present-day Bluff and the San Juan River valley. Some of its lower walls were found to be solidly constructed of core and veneer—trimmed sandstone blocks encasing a rubble core. The building includes at least one kiva. Like many others, this great house is enclosed by several middens (refuse mounds) and berms. Openings through the mounds may have been the entrances of ancient roads, or linear alignments on the landscape. Archaeologists have long known about roads leading in and out of Chaco Canyon and in recent years have recorded many more associated with dozens of great houses. Most are only a mile or two long, but a few continue long distances over the landscape.

In the first field season, the UC investigators uncovered ceramics revealing that the Bluff Great House was built in several phases between about A.D. 1000 and 1125, which was the height of Chaco's florescence. Other findings, however, show that the berms may have been built later, indicating that this great house remained in use long after Chaco's demise.

The excavators noted that some of the pottery they found, which was locally made, closely resembled in style the pottery being made and used in Chaco Canyon at the same time. Since Chaco Canyon was too far away (125 miles) to safely transport pots, it seems the local Bluff folks did the best they could: they made copies. And so the nature of the Chaco-Bluff relationship begins to reveal itself.

The great kiva adjacent to Bluff Great House—it appears today as a depression in the ground—also has some unusual, though not unique, features. Its wall surrounds an interior circular space, forty-two feet in diameter, which probably was used for ceremonies and/or community gatherings. Several rooms are attached to the exterior of the kiva wall. For the present, their function is unknown, but future excavations at the site may reveal how they were once used.

While the great house at this site clearly is Chacoan, researchers found evidence of a much earlier occupation, with construction possibly beginning around A.D. 400. Thus, people may have lived on this spot off and on for eight hundred years or longer.

Bluff Great House serves as a training ground for archaeology students at the University of Colorado. They learn how to plan and design a research project and conduct field and laboratory work. One relatively new technique the students have been exposed to at Bluff Great House has been ground-penetrating radar, a way to identify and map subsurface architectural features while avoiding the costly, destructive process of excavation. The students also met representatives from several southwestern Indian tribes, who were invited to visit the site and give their perspectives on its history.

Bluff Great House is privately owned but managed by the Southwest Heritage Foundation, which has developed a self-guided interpretive trail around the site. You will find accommodations, restaurants, and other travel services in Bluff. This is a good jumping-off place to see Hovenweep National Monument (p. 67) and Monument Valley, or take a rafting trip on the San Juan River (p. 91).

Suggested reading: "The Prehistoric People of San Juan County, Utah," by Winston Hurst, in *San Juan County, Utah: People, Resources, History*, edited by Allen Kent Powell, Utah State Historical Society, Salt Lake City, Utah, 1983.

# San Juan River

*The San Juan River rises in the mountains of south-central Colorado, dips into northwestern New Mexico, bends north to flow past the Four Corners into southeastern Utah, and continues west to Lake Powell, where its waters mingle with those of the Colorado River. Information: (435) 587-1532.*

As the principal drainage of the Colorado Plateau, the San Juan River and its tributaries were the cradle of ancestral Pueblo or Anasazi culture. Like all human beings, the Anasazi depended upon the presence of water for their survival and most of their religious ceremonies were an appeal for rain.

Many major Indian ruins can be found along the San Juan River and its tributaries, such as the Animas and Piedra rivers and Chinle and Chaco washes. Sites such as Aztec Ruins (p. 128), Pueblo Bonito (p. 114), and Chimney Rock Pueblo (p. 135) are in formal parks accessible by car. But there are other sites that you can reach only by raft or canoe. These include cliff houses, undisturbed pueblo mounds, and outstanding panels of petroglyphs. The difficulty, however, is knowing where to look, understanding and appreciating what you are seeing, and managing the travel logistics.

A number of river rafting companies operate recreational float trips down the San Juan River between Montezuma Creek, Utah, and Lake Powell. The most rewarding stretch of river for prehistory buffs, however, lies between Bluff and Mexican Hat. Wild Rivers Expeditions (800/422-7654) in Bluff, Utah, specializes in educational rafting trips on the San Juan River, where as much time can be spent seeing archaeological sites off the river as floating through the canyons.

Archaeological sites that you will see on a river-rafting trip include the Moki Steps Site, cliff dwellings such as River House and Floating House, and the Butler Wash petroglyph panel with its many impressive Basketmaker II anthropomorphic figures. Near River House you can also see the remains of a Mormon trading post dating to the 1880s. Other interesting sites up side canyons can be visited, too, when accompanied by a knowledgeable guide.

Archaeology aside, a float down the San Juan River is a memorable experience. This fast-moving but gentle river runs through quiet pastoral countryside before it enters steep-walled canyons with dramatic geologic formations. You will see a variety of desert flora and possibly lizards, waterfowl, beavers, bighorn sheep, and other wildlife. At night, you will be amazed by the brilliance of the stars.

Rafting companies offer trips from one day to a week in length. They provide all equipment, as well as professional guides who row the rafts, lead hikes, prepare meals, and are trained in first aid. Trip arrangements can be made directly with a river company or by signing on with tours

*Ancient carved steps lead up a cliff along the San Juan River.*

sponsored by an organization such as The Archaeological Conservancy, (505/266-1540), which offer educational programs along the way.

You will find overnight accommodations, restaurants, and other travel services in Bluff. Some establishments, such as Recapture Lodge and Pioneer House Bed and Breakfast, offer guided excursions to points of interest. Natural Bridges National Monument (p. 85), Hovenweep National Monument (p. 67), and Monument Valley are within easy reach of Bluff.

> Suggested reading: *San Juan Canyons: A River Runner's Guide,* by Don Baars and Gene Stevenson, Canon Publishers Ltd., Evergreen, Colorado, 1986.

# Sand Island Petroglyph Site

*The Sand Island Petroglyph Site is along a cliff bordering the San Juan River three miles west of Bluff, Utah, off Highway 163/191. The turnoff to the site is well marked. Information: (435) 587-1532.*

Thousands of rock art sites can be found throughout the Southwest. Some are solitary pictographs or petroglyphs, or others are groups or panels of images. The Sand Island site is one of the most extensive collections that you can find anywhere and one of the most easily accessible, too. It includes pictures from late Archaic and early Basketmaker times, the Pueblo period, and the nineteenth and twentieth centuries.

The glyphs appear along a long cliff of Navajo sandstone facing the San Juan River. Weathering causes the exposed surface of rock to acquire an ever-darkening patina, sometimes called desert varnish. At Sand Island, not only is the cliff surface blackened, but many of the petroglyphs have grown darkly repatinated, too, a clue to their considerable age.

You will recognize Basketmaker II anthropomorphic figures here, dating to pre-agricultural times, by their husky trapezoidal torsos and broad shoulders and the crescent shapes above their heads. A few even earlier markings made in the Glen Canyon Linear Style are visible, too, high up on the panel. They are small figures with vertical lines and antennae on their heads. Later Pueblo images and designs are well represented, including bighorn sheep and many renditions of the flute player, sometimes called Kokopelli, noted for his humped back and erect phallus. This ancient personage, surrounded by lore and legend, is still important in Pueblo mythology and religion today.

You will note historic pictures, too, including horses and riders, which are the product of Ute and Navajo Indians. One naturally wonders how people managed to peck their pictures so high up. A brownish scar on the cliff face offers a clue: at one time, sand dunes were piled high

*Depiction of Kokopelli, the humpbacked flute player, at Sand Island.*

against the cliff. To achieve even further height, glyph makers used ladders and scaffolding.

Binoculars will help you see many of the Sand Island petroglyphs. As the panel tends to glare in the sun, early-morning picture taking is recommended for the best results. A cyclone fence has been erected here to protect the panel from vandalism.

Near the petroglyphs is a small, rustic, attractive campground, as well as a popular boat-launching site for river runners. You can arrange to see other archaeological sites along the river (p. 91) by joining a raft trip with Wild Rivers Expeditions in nearby Bluff. The town also has motels, restaurants, gas stations, and a market. While in this area, you may enjoy driving to Valley of the Gods, Goosenecks State Park, and Monument Valley.

# Navajo National Monument

*Navajo National Monument is located in northeastern Arizona. To reach it, follow U.S. 160 northeast for 50 miles from Tuba City or southwest for 22 miles from Kayenta. At this point, a 9-mile paved road (Arizona 564) leads to the monument's visitor center. Information: (520) 672-2366.*

From a distance, the magnificent cliff dwellings of Kiet Siel and Betatakin in Navajo National Monument appear tiny and fragile against the vaulted rock alcoves that shelter them. Located in a remote canyon-cut sector of the Navajo reservation, they are two of the largest and best preserved cliff houses in the Southwest. (Both require some planning and commitment of time and energy to fully appreciate them.)

The Kayenta Anasazi inhabitants of these sites, like their Mesa Verdean and Chacoan neighbors to the east, were farmers, builders, and craftsmen. In the 1100s and 1200s, the Kayenta culture extended west to the Grand Canyon, east to the Chuska Mountains, north into southern Utah, and south to the Hopi Mesas.

Built in the 1260s and 1270s, Betatakin and Kiet Siel were occupied for only a couple of generations. During the latter part of the thirteenth century some Anasazi consolidated their scattered communities into large protected and defensive sites. Some cliff sites, like Betatakin and Kiet Siel, were located close to springs, but others sacrificed such convenience and are found perched on almost inaccessible mesa tops. Most of these sites are located within or on the edge of a maze of sinuous canyons. During this period, what was going on?

Archaeologists theorize that many Anasazi communities were experiencing food shortages caused by a prolonged drought and concomitant erosion of farmlands caused by a pattern of severe summer thunderstorms. Competition for limited food resources may have given rise to conflict, motivating groups of people to draw together for mutual defense. Whether or not open warfare occurred is uncertain, but even the threat of it could have caused new social patterns to emerge. By A.D. 1300, these local problems had been resolved by emigration.

## Betatakin

From the visitor center you can walk to an overlook to view Betatakin. Binoculars are useful. In the summer season, a daily ranger-guided hiking tour is conducted to the site, weather permitting. Reservations are on a first-come, first served basis. The hike, parts of which are strenuous, takes about five hours. Call the monument about the current schedule.

Betatakin, which means "ledge house" in Navajo, lies under the shelter of a five hundred foot cliff overhang and looks out over a narrow canyon with stands of scrub oak, aspen, and pine trees. When summer showers send thin waterfalls over the cliff from the slickrock mesa above not a drop of water touches the ancient Anasazi dwellings. Betatakin was planned and constructed as an entire unit, then occupied by a single group of people. The seven hundred-year-old houses are remarkably well preserved, some with roofs and ceilings intact.

When the site was discovered by John Wetherill and Byron Cummings in 1907, it contained a huge assortment of artifacts. Navajos living nearby had long avoided the ruins, believing them to be haunted by spirits of the dead. This superstition no doubt contributed to the site's fine preservation.

## Kiet Siel

To reach Kiet Siel you will need strong walking legs, a reservation, and a backcountry permit. The scenic eight-mile hike through Navajo lands leads down a switchback trail into Tsegi Canyon and up Kiet Siel Canyon. Once there, you can camp overnight below the ruins and return the next day. Of course, you must carry your own food, water, and camping equipment. Kiet Siel normally is open only from Memorial Day to Labor Day and only ten people are allowed access each day. Call well ahead for reservations.

This cliff dwelling was first recorded by Richard Wetherill, a Mancos, Colorado, rancher who earlier had explored sites on Mesa Verde. The pueblo has 155 rooms and six kivas, which look out over a quiet valley. An intermittent stream flows through a meadow and past a grove of cottonwood trees, where the campground is located. Kiet Siel's fine preservation gives the impression of its inhabitants having left much more recently than seven centuries ago. By tree-ring dating its many intact roof beams researchers were able to reconstruct a room-by-room building sequence for the entire pueblo.

The monument has a visitor center with archaeological exhibits, an educational slide program, picnic sites, and a campground. Two short scenic hikes are available without permits or guides. During summer months, rangers offer campfire talks on the area's history and natural

*Kiet Siel, Navajo National Monument.*

*Pictographs in Turkey Cave near Kiet Siel Ruins.*

environment. Travel services are available fifteen miles away along Highway 160 and in the town of Kayenta. Do not miss Monument Valley while you are touring this area.

> Suggested reading: "The Evolution of the Kayenta Anasazi," by Jonathan Haas, in *Houses Beneath the Rock: Canyon de Chelly and Navajo National Monument,* edited by David Grant Noble, Ancient City Press, Santa Fe, New Mexico, 1986.

## Canyon de Chelly National Monument

*Canyon de Chelly National Monument is located 3 miles from Route 191 in Chinle, in northeastern Arizona. Information: (520) 674-5500.*

Long ago, the Rio de Chelly cut through the colorful sandstone of northern Arizona's plateau country to form an exquisite canyon. Looking over the canyon's rim, you will see a glistening thread of water—though it can be a raging torrent—meandering through cottonwood groves and sandbars and flowing past Navajo farms. Canyon de Chelly has the deserved reputation of being one of the most scenic corners of the Southwest.

Chelly, pronounced "shay," is a Hispanicized version of the Navajo word *tseyi,* loosely translating as "canyon." With its sister, Canyon del Muerto, it has nurtured life for thousands of years. Between A.D. 1050 and 1300, however, human habitation here reached a peak with the building of dramatic cliff dwellings, including White House, Antelope

House, and Mummy Cave. Both canyons also contain impressive panels of pictographs and petroglyphs from the Basketmaker, Pueblo, and Navajo periods.

Attracted by the presence of water and natural shelters, Canyon de Chelly's first permanent residents were pithouse-dwelling Basketmakers between A.D. 300 and 420. After A.D. 550, they began to practice agriculture, make pottery, use the bow and arrow, and live in sizeable pithouse villages. Many of their sites have been found in rock shelters such as Mummy Cave, Big Cave, and Battle Cove, buried beneath the layers of later Pueblo settlements.

The Pueblo period, when the Anasazi of Canyon de Chelly started building above-ground masonry homes, began around A.D. 700 and continued until the late 1200s. Archaeological surveys have shown that the canyon's population remained modest for several centuries, then increased sharply after A.D. 1050, partly due to immigration. The Indians expanded Antelope House and Mummy Cave to accommodate more occupants and began construction of White House, Battle Cove, and Ledge Ruin. In addition, more settlements were founded on the plateau outside the canyon.

After A.D. 1150, many people left their plateau villages to live in cliff dwellings. Why cliff dwellings? Some scholars point out that in addition to providing excellent shelter, they were effective as defense against external attack. Also, they allowed people to move off land in the flood plain needed for cultivation. Most cliff dwellings face south, and thus

*Mummy Cave in Canyon del Muerto.*

*Navajo pictograph of Spanish cavalcade in Canyon de Chelly.*

are warmed by the winter sun while being shaded in summer.

Sometime in the 1200s, people began to move away and by 1284, Mummy Cave, the last occupied village in the canyon system, was vacant. Theories abound for why the Anasazi abandoned the Four Corners region; drought, pestilence, warfare, and social disruption frequently are cited. Since one problem usually leads to another, the truth probably lies in all explanations.

To the Hopi Indians, who live only fifty miles away, some sites in Canyon de Chelly are sacred; Hopi legends say that the Hisatsinom, or ancestors, once lived here and ceramic evidence supports these narratives.

In the early 1700s, Navajo Indians moved into Canyon de Chelly and Canyon del Muerto. These people, who appeared in the Southwest sometime after A.D. 1450, had been living in a region called Dinetah (p. 223), but pressures from Spanish colonization in New Mexico began pushing them westward. Sometimes the Navajos traded with the Pueblo and Spanish settlements of the Rio Grande region; other times, they raided these neighbors to obtain food, horses, sheep, and even human captives. Canyon de Chelly eventually became a Navajo stronghold. In 1805, Lt. Antonio Narbonna led a punitive expedition into the canyon and trapped many Navajos in a rock shelter. Because of the 115 Indians who perished there, the site would later be called Massacre Cave. The Spanish cavalcade is depicted in an impressive pictograph above

Standing Cow Ruins.

Sixty-one years after Narbonna, another soldier led cavalry troops into Canyon de Chelly. He was Col. Kit Carson and his mandate was to subdue the Navajos once and for all by forcing them onto a reservation in eastern New Mexico. Carson's soldiers brought the de Chelly Navajos to submission by burning their homes and destroying their food stores and orchards. The Indians' subsequent incarceration at Fort Sumner lasted until 1868 when they signed a treaty with the United States and returned to their homeland.

A small number of Navajos still have homes within Canyon de Chelly and Canyon del Muerto, where they farm, tend orchards, and keep flocks of sheep. In fact, the National Park Service manages the monument in close cooperation with the Navajo Nation. Many more Navajos live and work in the town of Chinle.

The quickest, easiest way to experience Canyon de Chelly is to drive the rim roads and stop at scenic overlooks. At White House Overlook, a mile-and-a-quarter length trail leads to White House Ruins. The hike, which takes about 45 minutes to get there, and a bit longer to come back, is your only opportunity to hike on your own in the canyon. The Park Service, however, offers other guided walking tours and natural history programs at scheduled times.

Thunderbird Lodge (520/674-5841), located in the park, conducts guided driving tours up the canyons. By hiring a Navajo guide, you can also explore the canyons in your own four-wheel drive, high-clearance vehicle. Call the Park Service for information about personal guides, group hikes, and horseback trips.

The monument has a campground and picnic sites, and Chinle has several motels and eateries as well as a supermarket and gas stations. While you are in this area, a visit to Hubbell Trading Post National Historic Site is highly recommended.

Suggested reading: *Canyon de Chelly: Its People and Rock Art,* by Campbell Grant, University of Arizona Press, Tucson, Arizona, 1978.

*View of Grand Canyon from the South Rim.*

## Grand Canyon National Park

*Grand Canyon National Park is accessible from its south or north rims. The South Rim is located along Arizona 64, 57 miles north of Interstate 40 at Williams, Arizona. The North Rim headquarters are at the end of Arizona 67, 44 miles south of Jacob Lake. The North Rim is closed from mid-October to mid-May. Information: (520) 638-7888. Entrance fee.*

Grand Canyon is a picture window into time past. Its many layers of colorful rock, descending thousands of feet to the Colorado River, represent the hours of a regressive clock whose hands move slower than the human mind can comprehend. Within its long hour of geologic time, Grand Canyon's human story accounts for but seconds.

Archaeologists have discovered a rare type of artifact buried in cysts in caves in the canyon. Known as split-twig figurines, they are small effigies of mountain sheep and deer, carefully crafted of split and twisted willow and cottonwood twigs, sometimes also using grass or bark. Some are pierced by tiny spears. The figurines are thought to have been fetishes used in hunting rituals by Archaic-era people who roamed these canyons and mesas some four thousand years ago.

*Split-willow twig figurines from a Grand Canyon cave.*

Small groups of Basketmaker people began using Grand Canyon about A.D. 500, and by A.D. 700, a few farming settlements had been established on the South Rim. Within two more centuries, the North Rim was settled, too. About A.D. 1050, large numbers of ancestral Pueblo farmers began to establish communities near arable deltas within the canyon and on its rims. Alternating their residence seasonally between the two areas, which have a 5,600-foot elevation differential, gave these farmers the advantage of a long growing season.

Archaeologists have found many Anasazi sites in and around Grand Canyon dating to between A.D. 1050 and 1150. By 1200 or so, the Indians had departed from here, probably migrating eastward to the area of the Hopi Mesas. The Hopi village of Oraibi, indeed, was founded at just about this time. Grand Canyon remains an important place in Hopi mythology and religion and members of this tribe still return to visit a mineral spring, which they believe was their original place of emergence into the present world. Three Grand Canyon archaeological sites are open to visitors.

## Tusayan Ruin

Tusayan Ruin, located on the South Rim between Grand Canyon Village and Desert View, is a small, unimposing site consisting of the remains of a few living and storage rooms and a kiva. Built toward the end of the 1100s, this pueblo housed about thirty people, who lived here for only two generations before moving on. The site was excavated in the 1930s by the noted archaeologist, Emil W. Haury. Today, a self-guided interpretive trail leads through the ruins. In addition, a small museum further enhances your understanding of Grand Canyon's human past.

*Tusayan Ruin, of the South Rim.*

## Walhalla Glades Ruin

The Walhalla Glades Ruin on the North Rim, which is closed in winter, is located across the road from the Walhalla Glades Overlook, twenty-four miles from Grand Canyon Lodge and two miles from Cape Royal. It is a small house that probably sheltered a single family after A.D. 1050. The Indians at Walhalla Glades probably moved into the inner canyon in winter to avoid the frigid temperatures and deep snows of the North Rim's eight-thousand-foot elevation. Archaeological investigations were conducted here and at other nearby sites in 1960 and 1970 by the School of American Research.

## Bright Angel Pueblo

When John Wesley Powell explored Grand Canyon in 1869, he commented on and named this site. Located along the Kaibab Trail about a hundred yards from the north end of the Colorado River footbridge, this site is accessible only to inner canyon hikers. Indians built a pithouse here about A.D. 1050 but were forced away by drought fifteen years later. Around 1100, however, several families moved back, built a small pueblo, cultivated a garden, and managed to sustain themselves until about 1140. Then they left for good. Distances to this site by way of the Kaibab and Bright Angel trails are seven and nine miles, respectively, and it is a fourteen-mile hike from the North Rim. Camping and overnight accommodations are available by reservation at nearby Phantom Ranch.

Any commentary on Grand Canyon's human history should include mention of the Havasupai Indians, who have lived in the western section of the canyon along Havasu Creek for untold generations. In prehistoric and early historic times, the life of these Indians in the canyon and on the South Rim was similar to that of the Anasazi centuries before. Today, they lead a quiet rural life in their isolated valley, the last community in North America to receive regular mail delivery by pack train.

Another group of American Indians identified with Grand Canyon are various bands of Southern Paiutes, who migrated here around A.D. 1400. These nomadic foragers followed a seasonal cycle in which they exploited a wide variety of plant foods and hunted small game. In the eighteenth and nineteenth centuries, Paiute women and children were regularly taken as captives by Utes and Navajos and later by Spaniards and Americans to be sold in New Mexico and California as slaves. They later lost their lands to ranchers and experienced a drastic decline in population. Today, the descendants of these Indians live on a series of tiny reservations to the north and west of Grand Canyon.

Scientific research in Grand Canyon has understandably focused on the region's fascinating geology and natural history. Not much archaeology was done here until recent decades. Even then, the environment and topography have made it a challenging enterprise. Excavation crews at Unkar Delta in the late 1960s, for example, contended with daytime temperatures above 120 degrees and depended upon helicopters to deliver food and supplies. The archaeologists appreciated the fact that Grand Canyon's challenging environment made it a true Anasazi frontier, where life was tenuous and where viable villages of one decade might lie as silent ghost towns the next.

Suggested reading: *On the Edge of Splendor: Exploring Grand Canyon's Human Past*, by Douglas W. Schwartz, School of American Research Press, Santa Fe, New Mexico, 1989.

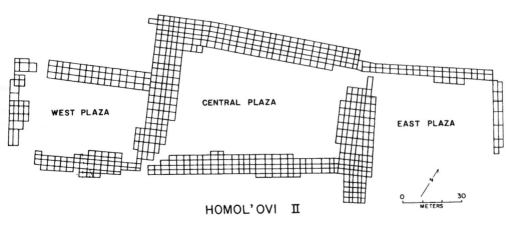

WEST PLAZA

CENTRAL PLAZA

EAST PLAZA

HOMOL'OVI  II

0 _____ 30
METERS

*Plan of Homol'ovi II ruins.*

# Homol'ovi Ruins State Park

*Homol'ovi Ruins State Park is three miles northeast of Winslow, Arizona. From Interstate 40, take Exit 257 and follow Arizona 87 north 1.3 miles to the park's entrance. Information: (520) 289-4106. Entrance fee.*

North of Winslow, Arizona, lies the reservation of the Hopi Indians. According to their beliefs, when their ancestors, the Hisatsinom, (also known as the Anasazi) emerged into the present world from a world beneath, they spent a period of time wandering about in search of a new homeland. During this era, the Hisatsinom settled down temporarily in various locations, including places that have since been set aside as national parks and monuments: Canyon de Chelly (p. 98), Wupatki (p. 148), and Tuzigoot (p. 163), are some examples. Another is Homol'ovi—in the Hopi language, *homol* means "butte(s)" and *ovi,* "place of."

Homol'ovi Ruins State Park contains more than 340 archaeological sites, including the remains of several large pueblos. As ancestral homes, these sites are sacred to the Hopi, while to archaeologists, they represent a rich resource for information about the past. Investigations of the ruins, therefore, have been a collaboration.

The first excavations of Homol'ovi were made in 1896 by Jesse Walter Fewkes. When he consulted the Hopis about their connection to these ruins, he learned that they had oral traditions telling of named Hopi clans whose ancestors once lived at Homol'ovi. Stories about the pueblo's founding and abandonment also were told.

In 1984, archaeologists and students from the University of Arizona began doing research at Homol'ovi, a general aim being to reconstruct

*Petroglyph at Homol'ovi Ruins State Park.*

its cultural history. The ongoing project has resulted in a series of published volumes on the prehistory of the Homol'ovi area.

As E. Charles Adams and his colleagues reconstruct Homol'ovi's past, the Hisatsinom first lived here, probably on a seasonal basis, between A.D. 750 and 850. During this period, which was wetter than normal, they resided in small pithouse hamlets and dry-farmed the sand dunes. Then, when the weather turned dryer, they moved away, possibly to the north to the Hopi Mesas area. Two centuries later, some of their descendants came back to renew life along the Little Colorado River.

After A.D. 1250, Homol'ovi's population grew markedly. This was a period of much movement and migration among the Four Corners Anasazi. The Homol'ovi folk built at least seven small hamlets on the east side of the river to be followed by two pueblos, Homol'ovi III and IV, on the west side. They liked this area because of its reliable water supply, excellent farming potential along the river, and good hunting.

Soon after 1300, the west bank pueblos were abandoned, their occupants moving across the river. At the same time, the residents of small hamlets were aggregating into much larger pueblos, including Homol'ovi I, with two hundred-fifty rooms, and Homol'ovi II, with more than a thousand. People farmed the river's floodplain as well as the dunes, valleys, and upland areas. Corn, of course, was their staple, but they also raised a variety of beans, squashes and gourds, and lots of cotton, which they bartered with neighbors for pottery, obsidian, and other goods. While they hunted large game such as deer and antelope, their main source of meat protein came from rabbits, which they probably killed in organized hunting drives much as the Hopi did in historic times. The Homol'ovi area did not lend itself to making pottery, probably due to a lack of fuel suitable for firing ceramics, Much of the pottery used by the Homol'ovi folk—a distinctive yellow ware--was imported from the Hopi area, especially the town of Awatovi, fifty miles to the north.

As the Homol'ovi people increased, their society became more organized, especially in the way it controlled land use. This new organization is reflected in the arrangement of pueblos around a central plaza, where people worked and held communal religious ceremonies. After A.D. 1325, the iconography of pottery decorations and rock art reflects the appearance of the kachina cult, a complex of religious practices that remains active among the Hopis and other Pueblo Indians today. In the late 1300s, Homol'ovi society was no longer thriving as it had and by the early 1400s, the area was abandoned, this time for good. No one returned to live here until Mormon settlers arrived in the late nineteenth century.

It goes without saying that the Southwest's prehistoric farming communities were extremely sensitive to even minor shifts in climatic and environmental conditions. As archaeologists reconstruct the settlements and abandonments of the Homol'ovi villages, one key factor was having just the right amount of water in the Little Colorado River, a nearly perennial stream. Too much flow and floodplain farming became impossible; too little, and agriculture declined.

Another factor in Homol'ovi's economic success was participation in an active trade network that reached far in all directions. In addition to trading cotton, residents took advantage of an abundance of natural resources in their riverine environment—plants, bird feathers, and turtles, for example—that were highly marketable to communities located in dryer upland areas.

In 1991, Homol'ovi was opened as a state park, with an interpretive program, visitor center and museum, and campground. When you come, stop first at the visitor center for general information and directions to the ruins and nearby petroglyph sites.

In addition to assisting visitors, an important function of the park is to protect these sites from looting, which has been a huge problem in the past at Homol'ovi. Your first view of the cratered landscape around Homol'ovi II, may remind you of pictures of a World War I battlefield. The craters are, in fact, pothunters' holes. Looting on federal land is a federal crime (p. 227) as well as an act that robs us all of a portion of our heritage and causes special injury to Native Americans.

You will find travel services in Winslow. If you are headed west on Interstate 40, do not miss an opportunity to see Walnut Canyon

National Monument (p. 151), a place of much archaeological and scenic appeal.

Suggested reading: *Kiva*, vol. 54, no. 3, Arizona Archaeological and Historical Society, Tucson, Arizona, 1989.

# Petrified Forest National Park

*Petrified Forest National Park is located along Interstate 40, 25 miles east of Holbrook, Arizona, and along U.S. 180, 19 miles east of Holbrook. Information: (520) 524-6228. Entrance fee.*

Petrified Forest, in east-central Arizona, has the largest and most colorful collection of fossilized trees in the world. In this unique desert park, you can walk through a series of toppled fossil forests where giant agate logs litter the surface of the ground, relics of an age that antedates the presence of the human species in the Southwest by millions of years.

This desolate region, whose beauty lies in the rich colorations of its sands and clays, does not appear to hold much potential for human habitation. Archaeological research here, however, bears evidence to the contrary. On these mesas, along drainages, and around springs and seeps, are cultural sites of great antiquity.

The oldest remains are hunter-gatherer campsites, thousands of years old. Archaic Indians, who pursued a seminomadic existence living off a wide variety of wild plants and animals, came here on a seasonal basis, probably revisiting their same camps year after year. Of particular interest to them, and to everyone who followed, was the colorful petrified wood from which excellent projectile points could be chipped.

After knowledge of agriculture spread into the American Southwest, raising corn began to supplement foraging. By A.D. 300 to 500, a few early Basketmaker people were living in the uplands, probably on a seasonal basis. Their homes were shallow, slab-lined pithouses with dome-like roofs made of sticks, brush, and mud supported by poles. By A.D. 700, farming methods had become more productive and many of the area's inhabitants were living in larger pithouse villages. Above-ground masonry dwellings or pueblos did not appear in the Petrified Forest area until after A.D. 900. At this time, increased rainfall combined with better farming techniques, including simple water-control systems, had allowed people to plant gardens in many parts of the landscape. Sand dune areas were especially successful due to their moisture retention advantages.

One archaeological site that is easily accessible—it is located along Mainline Road—is the Puerco Ruin. This pueblo was founded in the mid-1200s, when the Anasazi inhabitants of the region were coming together in a few larger villages. It consists of 125 single-story rooms built around a rectangular courtyard with three kivas. From their

*Petroglyphs at Petrified Forest.*

rooftops, its two hundred inhabitants had a view over the Puerco River and surrounding landscape.

The people of Puerco Pueblo sustained themselves by farming along the river's floodplain, hunting rabbits and prairie dogs, gathering native plants, and trading. The abundance of chipped stone artifacts in and around the site, (mostly petrified wood) lead researchers to believe that tool manufacture was a central activity here. Imported pottery found at this and other Petrified Forest sites shows that these Indians enjoyed an active prehistoric trade with the ancestral Hopis and Zunis, as well as with towns such as Kinishba (p. 111) in the White Mountains to the south. Why everyone left Puerco Pueblo is unclear. Some inhabitants apparently dribbled away over the years, then in about 1380, the remaining families abruptly set fire to their homes and departed.

When you visit this site, be sure to allow time to explore the large collection of petroglyphs scattered on rocks and boulders around the south and east sides of the mesa. Numbering more than eight hundred, the pictures depict human-like figures, animals, birds, kachina masks, hands, paws, and geometric designs. More clusters of glyphs can be found across Mainline Road on the opposite side of the mesa and at nearby Newspaper Rock.

Another easily accessible site, in the south end of the park, is Agate House. Reconstructed in 1934, this small prehistoric pueblo was built of chunks of petrified wood.

Petrified Forest was first reported in 1851 by Lt. Lorenzo Sitgreaves while on a U.S. Army exploratory expedition in northern Arizona. After the building of the railroad in the 1880s, this bleak country saw an influx of tourists, souvenir hunters, and gem collectors. In 1905 and 1906, the conservationist John Muir came here with his ailing daughter, hoping that the dry air would cure her, and became interested in the area's Indian ruins and natural resources. He excavated portions of the Puerco Ruin, but regretably did not record his findings. More importantly, he became concerned by the environmental impact of a nearby stamp mill that was crushing petrified logs for abrasives and helped convince President Theodore Roosevelt to declare Petrified Forest a national monument.

You can obtain an introduction to Petrified Forest's geology and cultural history at the park's visitor center. The main road passes by some of the best-known cultural and fossil-wood sites. If you wish to explore more remote area's of the park, you will need to obtain a permit from park officials. To see the visitor center, Puerco Ruin and its petroglyphs, and Agate House, you should plan on spending three or four hours in the park. The nearest travel services are in Holbrook.

Suggested reading: *Tapamveni: The Rock Art Galleries of Petrified Forest and Beyond,* by Patricia McCreery and Ekkehart Malotki.

# Kinishba Ruins

*To find Kinishba Ruins, drive 15 miles west of Whiteriver, Arizona, on Arizona 73 to the Kinishba Ruins sign on the highway. Turn right and continue about four miles to the site, which is signed. Information: (520) 338-4625.*

Like so many archaeological sites, Kinishba was first reported in the early 1880s by Adolph F. Bandelier, an anthropologist and historian who explored extensively in the Southwest. Half a century later, after much pothunting at the site by U.S. soldiers stationed at nearby Fort Apache, a large portion of Kinishba was excavated and restored by a crew of University of Arizona students and Apache Indians under the supervision of Byron Cummings. Much of the original pueblo, however, has never been submitted to shovel and trowel and remains as overgrown mounds.

Cummings selected Kinishba for excavation because he thought it represented "the highest development of the Pueblo culture," a claim to which other scholars may take exception. The wealth of artifacts he collected here during nine summers of field work, however, do testify to the highly developed craft skills of the Anasazi. The collection also demonstrates the heterogeneous character of Kinishba's culture. Kinishba's inhabitants exchanged ideas and goods with all their neigh-

*Reconstructed Kinishba building.*

bors: Kayenta Anasazi communities to the north, Tularosa people to the east, the Hopi villages of Sikyatki and Awatovi, and Salado and Hohokam traders from the lower Salt and Gila drainages to the south.

Kinishba was inhabited for three hundred years, from about A.D. 1050 to 1350. The people lived by farming corn, beans, and squash on arable lands sloping southeast to the White River. It was a large village with several substantial community houses built of stone. One of these buildings was the focus of Cummings's 1930s project. The pueblo was built on top of an older, collapsed village, and numerous pithouses are evidence of an even older Basketmaker occupation. Prehistoric southwestern peoples had a propensity for reoccupying previously inhabited sites, often constructing new homes on top of the ruins of older structures. Kinishba's roomblocks were well built and compact. The excavated wing had over two hundred rooms, and the entire pueblo may have had a population of fifteen hundred to two thousand people. Cummings was of the opinion that this large, productive, long-lived village must have had a strong sociopolitical organization with effective leadership.

At the end of Cummings's scientific investigations of Kinishba, he built a research and exhibition complex that he envisioned would be the core of a model educational park. He hoped that, in time, professional and lay people would come here to tour the site, relax under shade trees in a park, see Kinishba's art and artifact collections in a modern museum, and enjoy a contemporary Native American arts-and-crafts center.

Regrettably, World War II diverted public interest and funding away from projects like this and Cummings's dream of creating a cultural center ended. Today, Kinishba is deteriorating, barely known to the general public, and visited by few. To the serious archaeology student, however, this site represents an important example of Western Pueblo culture and should not be forgotten.

Kinishba Ruins are administered by the Fort Apache Tribe, which does not require special permission or a permit to visit the site. As a matter of safety, however, tribal officials strongly advise you to stay well clear of the ruins' highly unstable stone walls. When you go to Kinishba, you will be pretty much on your own and will find little interpretation and no facilities. If you pick up an artifact, be sure to put it back where you found it. You will find travel services in Springerville and Globe.

> Suggested reading: *Kinishba: A Prehistoric Pueblo of the Great Pueblo Period,* by Byron Cummings, The University of Arizona, Tucson, Arizona, 1940.

# Chaco Culture National Historical Park

*Chaco Culture National Historical Park is located between Farmington and Grants, New Mexico. From New Mexico 44 to the north, take County Road 7900 (3 miles east of Nageezi) for 5 miles, then CR 7950 for 16 miles to the park entrance. From the south, turn on New Mexico 57 from Interstate 40 and proceed to Crownpoint. Two miles north of Crownpoint, turn right on Navajo 9 to a marked turnoff. From here a 21-mile stretch leads north to the visitor center. Both accesses to Chaco have unpaved sections. Information: (505) 786-7014. Entrance fee.*

The roads to Chaco Canyon traverse a rough, arid landscape of badlands, dry washes, rock outcroppings, and sparse desert vegetation. You cannot help but wonder how a major culture once thrived here. But as you proceed, you see flocks of sheep grazing and tire tracks branching off the road toward Navajo homes, where wisps of chimney smoke curl into the crisp, dry air. This inhospitable land can support people.

Chaco Canyon itself is a shallow rift, fifteen miles long and up to a mile wide, bordered by low mesa cliffs. It is deeply cut by the Chaco Wash, which seldom flows now. On either side of the wash lie the ruins of large multistoried masonry buildings, some excavated and stabilized or partially restored, others still mounds. Here, an Anasazi center once thrived, whose sphere of influence extended a hundred miles and more in all directions. Not surprisingly, what happened here nine hundred years ago is commonly referred to as the Chaco phenomenon. And yet, even after generations of archaeological research, the very nature of that phenomenon remains unclear.

*Doorways in Pueblo Bonito.*

One of the early excavation projects was carried out at Pueblo Bonito by the Hyde Exploring Expedition in the late 1890s. Since then, institutions that have sponsored research in the canyon include the University of New Mexico, the National Geographic Society, the Smithsonian, and the National Park Service. Despite formidable accumulations of data, however, many central questions remain about Chaco Canyon. How many people lived here and how did they sustain themselves? Why have so few burials been found? How was the labor force organized to build these monumental buildings or "great houses," and how were these linked to nearby and far-flung outlying communities such as Aztec (p. 128), Chimney Rock (p. 135), and Bluff Great House (p. 89)? In short, why was Chaco Canyon what it was, and what was it?

Although hunter-gatherers were familiar with Chaco Canyon and early Basketmaker horticulturalists lived here, the Pueblo period, which led to Chaco's present fame, did not begin until around A.D. 700. By 900, the canyon's population was growing and compact masonry pueblos were being built. One group lived in a curved suite of rooms near the north wall of the canyon, the first section of what would become the world-known Pueblo Bonito.

Chaco's most active building period began around 1030 and continued at a frenzied pace for several decades. Soon, Pueblo Bonito, Chetro Ketl, Pueblo del Arroyo, Pueblo Alto, and other structures were focal points of an Anasazi power center. By 1115, this power was manifested at scores of outlying communities, most of them marked by a Chacoan great house, roadway, great kiva, and other special features. Each outlier seemed to dominate a community of local farmers living in humble dwellings. Some scholars see the great houses as trading posts, others as the domiciles of powerful overlords, but everyone recognizes that they once had a religious and ceremonial dimension.

A curious aspect of the Chaco phenomenon are the associated roads. Two of these wide linearities radiate from Chaco Canyon to the north and south. The Great North Road heads toward Aztec. They are hard to see from ground level, but appear, ghostlike, in aerial photographs. At thirty feet across and highly engineered, they were more than trails. When a road encountered a topographical barrier such as a mesa, its builders did not circumvent it; instead, they built a ramp or staircase up and over. Many roads lead out from a great house complex for only a mile or so, then vanish. Did they mark the routes for ceremonial processions? Did they physically legitimize Chaco's power? Research on the roads continues; however, ideas about their purpose may forever lie in the realm of theory.

About A.D. 1140, the Chaco system fell apart. The outliers were abandoned first, then the canyon. The collapse coincided with diminished regional precipitation. If the rains failed, perhaps faith in the rain gods and priests did, too. New research strongly suggests a move of political power from Chaco to Aztec (p. 128) in the early 1100s. Anyone inter-

*Back wall of Chetro Ketl, Chaco Canyon.*

ested in studying the riddles of Chaco will find an abundance of published literature to read. One new provocative book, *The Chaco Meridian*, by Stephan H. Lekson, argues a Chaco–Aztec–Casas Grandes power sequence.

When you visit the canyon, Pueblo Bonito should be a top priority for its hundreds of rooms, many kivas, and fine masonry. Also walk around Chetro Ketl and see the great kiva at Casa Rinconada. There are other inner-canyon sites to visit, too, each with its own self-guiding brochure. If you have the time, you should take advantage of hiking trails to sites such as Peñasco Blanco, Pueblo Alto, and Wijiji. At the visitor center, you can obtain information about various trails and rules relating to archaeological protection.

How should you plan a visit to Chaco? At the minimum, spend half a day in the monument. For a fuller experience, however, drive there early in the morning with a picnic lunch and stay through late afternoon. If you are equipped, stay overnight at the campground; then you will catch the beauty of sunrise and sunset in this extraordinary place.

The park has a museum, toilets, and water fountain but no travel services or firewood. When you come here you should have food, water, appropriate clothing and footwear, and plenty of gas. Do not stray from designated trails or collect artifacts. Beware of dirt roads that turn to slick mud in wet weather. The nearest restaurants, grocery stores, and motels are in the Farmington and Gallup areas.

*Navajo petroglyph of ceremonial figure, Chaco Canyon.*

Suggested reading: *New Light on Chaco Canyon,* edited by David Grant Noble, School of American Research Press, Santa Fe, New Mexico, 1985.

# Casamero Pueblo

*To reach Casamero Pueblo, take the Prewitt exit from Interstate 40, 19 miles west of Grants, New Mexico. Turn right on Route 66, then north on County Road 19 and continue 4 miles to a small parking area on the left. A short foot trail leads to the ruins. Information: (505) 761-8700.*

Casamero is one of more than a hundred Chacoan outliers. Chaco Canyon (p. 113), located about fifty miles to the north, was an important Anasazi cultural and religious center that reached its peak between around A.D. 1040 and 1140. Although archaeologists are not quite sure how to define it, they recognize a close connection between the monumental sites in Chaco Canyon and Casamero and other outliers. The evidence of this here is apparent in site layout, architectural details, and the presence of a great kiva and two Chacoan roads.

The main feature you will see at Casamero is the great house, which dates to between A.D. 1000 and 1125. You can freely walk around this structure, whose walls stand about waist high. Excavations conducted

*Kiva entrance at Casamero.*

between 1966 and 1975 showed the building to contain twenty-two ground-floor rooms, six second-story rooms on the west side, and an interior kiva. The banded-masonry construction—large horizontally laid blocks of sandstone and limestone alternating with thin bands of chinking—is typically Chacoan in style.

Two hundred feet southeast of the Casamero great house lies an unexcavated great kiva, another Chacoan attribute. Appearing today as a large shallow depression in the ground, its diameter is conservatively estimated at seventy feet. This is almost twice the size of the great kiva at Aztec Ruins (p. 128) and even larger than the famous one at Casa Rinconada in Chaco Canyon. Its size suggests how populous this area once was.

To the east, Casamero was linked to another Chacoan outlier (not open to the public) by a road, and another road headed west from a point south of the great kiva. These features are nearly impossible to recognize from ground level. Archaeologists have been seriously studying and mapping Chacoan roads for about twenty years, and as more information has emerged, theories regarding their purpose have changed. Today, some scholars regard them as a type of ceremonial landscape expressing a belief system and manifesting Chacoan authority. They probably also served as routes for ritual processions.

In the 1970s, archaeologists from the School of American Research carried out extensive investigations near Casamero Pueblo, especially in the vicinity of the coal-fired electrical generating plant that you will pass along the way from Thoreau. They identified more than 140 archaeological sites in the vicinity, ranging from early Basketmaker pithouses to Puebloan structures to early twentieth-century Navajo homesteads. The valley's population today is probably smaller than at any time in its history. The Navajo sites included hogans, ramadas, sheep pens, and sweat lodges. At one home site, a tragedy apparently occurred in the not-too-distant past. Every structure excavated had been burned and even the melted remains of children's toys were dug from the scorched earth. Inquiries revealed that years ago, when this Navajo family had gone to town, their home, outbuildings, and corrals had been set afire.

The Bureau of Land Management, which administers Casamero Pueblo as a Chaco Culture Archaeological Protection Site, has placed interpretive signs around the ruins. The Bureau asks the public to report any evidence of theft or vandalism to its Albuquerque office at (505) 761-8700.

You will find travel services in Grants and in Gallup. To more fully understand Casamero's history, a visit to Chaco Canyon is highly recommended.

Suggested reading: *Anasazi Communities of the San Juan Basin,* by Michael P. Marshall, et al., Historic Preservation Bureau, Santa Fe, New Mexico, 1979.

# Dittert Site

*The Dittert Site is located several miles east of New Mexico 117, 42 miles south of Grants, New Mexico. To reach the site from Grants, drive 5 miles east on Interstate 40 and turn south on 117. Continue 9 miles to the Bureau of Land Management's El Malpais Ranger Station, where further directions to the site may be obtained. Information: (505) 783-4774.*

Mesa Verde and Montezuma Castle are ruins with mass appeal. The Dittert Site, on the other hand, is for the confirmed archaeology buff. Sites like this are well known to professional archaeologists and backcountry hikers, but to most people on a tight sightseeing itinerary, they are of limited interest.

This pueblo has around thirty rooms and a kiva. Archaeologist Alfred E. Dittert excavated and backfilled eight rooms and the kiva in the late

1940s. Today, what you find here is a substantial mound with several low-standing room walls made of sandstone blocks. The plaza was located in front of the kiva, outside the L-shaped room block. The existence of numerous other smaller pueblos and farmsteads in the vicinity suggest that this site was the focus of a more extensive prehistoric community.

Tree-ring samples taken at the Dittert Site date it to between A.D. 1226 and 1267; however, its residents built it on an earlier mound whose time period is unknown.

The Anasazi were drawn to this place, near the base of Cebolleta Mesa, for its good hunting and foraging and because waters flowing from Armijo Canyon and other drainages made farming possible. Two miles up the canyon, in fact, is a spring that the pueblo's occupants must have counted on in dry spells. More resources were available on *el malpais* (the badlands), a bit further to the west. Also to the west, a corridor between the badlands and Cebolleta Mesa would have served as a natural travel and trade route between the Dittert people and their neighbors.

Archaeologists have discussed whether or not this site was an outlier of Chaco Canyon. Some of its characteristics—masonry style, kiva features, and a nearby road segment—would so indicate. But it dates to seventy-five years after Chaco's collapse. Perhaps descendants of the Chacoans came here and continued to build in the style of their ancestors.

The Bureau of Land Management wants people to appreciate this ruin but needs to know when visitors are going there; please register at the El Malpais Ranger Station and act responsibly when exploring this remote place.

The nearest travel services are in Grants and Quemado. While here, you may wish to explore the geologically interesting and scenic El Malpais National Monument, and hike its Zuni–Acoma Trail (below). Another fascinating park in the vicinity is El Morro National Monument (p. 123).

# The Zuni–Acoma Trail

*The Zuni–Acoma Trail connected Zuni and Acoma pueblos in New Mexico. A segment of the old trail, which can be hiked, traverses El Malpais National Monument near Grants, New Mexico. On the west side of the monument, the trailhead begins on New Mexico 53, 16 miles south of Interstate 40. On the east side, it starts along New Mexico 117, 15 miles south of Interstate 40. There are visitor centers along both highways. Information: (505) 783-4774.*

An extensive network of trails crisscrossed the Southwest in ancient times. Many connected communities within a day's or several days' walk from each other; others linked widely separated cultural groups across hundreds of miles. Trails penetrating deep into Mexico to the south became corridors along which trade goods and ideologies reached the Southwest. Routes west saw an active commerce between the Anasazi

*View along the west end of the Zuni–Acoma Trail.*

and Hohokam and peoples on the Pacific Coast. Other major trails led north along the Rockies and west to the Great Plains.

It was the old Indian trails that Spanish and American explorers used when they explored the Southwest and the rest of the continent. While their joureys are legend and their fame justly deserved, it should be remembered that they had Indian guides and followed routes that already were older than collective human memory.

The Zuni–Acoma Trail, as its name implies, linked the pueblos of Zuni and Acoma. At Zuni it hooked up with other trails and from Acoma it continued to the Rio Grande Valley, which had a major trail of its own leading north and south. From the Rio Grande, you could branch northeast, as Coronado did, and reach the lands of the Witchitas and other Plains tribes.

Many Indian trails later developed into wagon roads, which eventually were leveled and widened to accomodate cars and even became interstate highways or railroad routes. A segment of the old Zuni–Acoma Trail, however, crossed the rugged *el malpais* (pronounced el-mal-pie-ees) south of Grants, New Mexico. This badland was created by eruptions from several nearby volcanos, one of which was Mount Taylor to the north. El Malpais is, in fact, a landscape of lava flows, some more than a million years old, others less than a thousand. This rough terrain is traversable by foot (often with difficulty), but tears up horses' hooves, as Spanish conquistadores discovered, and presents a formidable barrier to any wheeled vehicle. Because of its location in El Malpais National Monument, this section of the Zuni–Acoma Trail has been preserved.

The Acoma and Zuni Indians have myths about the *el malpais*. The Acomas say the black lava was blood, which flowed from the eyesockets of the kachina KauBat after he was blinded by his sons, the Twins, to punish him for his gambling. (Despite the apparent moral of this story, the Acoma Indains built a casino nearby in 1997.) The Indians maintain shrines deep within the badlands and regularly visit other sacred sites here that were used by their ancestors.

The lava flows harbor other sites, too. There are stone circles, whose function is unknown, rock cairns marking trails, agricultural features, petroglyphs, camping places, and even pueblos. Some intriguing features of the national monument are its lava tubes, ice caves, and frozen subterranean ponds. Archaeological evidence suggests that the temperatures of these places, even in summer, made them useful to the Indians for the cold storage of perishable agricultural goods. At one site, a cache of finely woven baskets was found. Regrettably, the artifacts from these places were stolen in years past, thus depriving us of potentially fascinating historical knowledge.

History and archaeology aside, the Zuni–Acoma Trail crosses a beautiful and highly unusual landscape. If you do even part of the trail, you will walk over grassy plains and meadows and a variety of old and new lava flows, pass sculptured sandstone formations, see dwarfed trees and cacti, and, if you are lucky, catch glimpses of melanistic forms of wildlife, including black frogs and squirrels. You will see lava tubes and lava bombs, pahoehoe lava and a'a lava, squeeze-ups and depressions, and, on the horizon, the cinder cones where all the lava came from.

If you want to experience the trail, keep in mind a few precautions. Spring and fall are the best hiking times, but cloudy summer or warm winter days also are feasible. Wear sturdy sneakers or boots and bring water, trail food, sunscreen, and hat. As it is seven miles from one side to the other, plan your schedule so as not to be looking for the way after dark and, if possible, avoid being caught here in a lightning storm. If you wish to try out the trail without committing to the full hike, walk in from one side or the other for a mile or two and retrace your steps. This method is especially convenient if you do not have a car awaiting you at the opposite end.

For more information on this and other trails in the area, consult the ranger staff at the two visitor centers, where you can also obtain a trail map and informational brochures. The town of Grants has motels, restaurants, and gas stations. Should you choose to take a short hike from the Route 53 side, you will have plenty of time to continue on to El Morro National Monument (p. 123), another interesting historical and archaeological park, also on the Zuni–Acoma Trail.

Suggested reading: *El Malpais National Monument,* by Marilyn Mabery, Southwest Parks and Monument Association, Tucson, Arizona, 1990.

*A famous message left at Inscription Rock: "Passed by here the Adelantado Don Juan de Oñate, from the discovery of the Sea of the South, the 16th of April of 1605."*

## El Morro National Monument

*El Morro National Monument is along New Mexico 53, 42 miles southwest of Grants and 30 miles east of Zuni, New Mexico. Information: (505) 783-4226. Entrance fee.*

The ancestral Zuni pueblo of Atsinna, which is perched on top of El Morro Mesa, has a bird's-eye view of the upper valley of the Zuni River. Below it lies Inscription Rock, resembling the prow of a great stone ship, on which are incised the names of Spanish conquistadores, explorers, and settlers. Some are famous, others known only by their signatures. At the base of the *morro*, which means "bluff" or "headland" in Spanish, a large pool collects runoff from the mesa. It was a popular camping place for Indians and Spaniards traveling from the Zuni pueblos to Acoma Pueblo and the Rio Grande Valley. While they relaxed here, they would inscribe their names, often with the date and a comment, on the face of the cliff. Over the generations, an intriguing folk-historic register was created.

Paleo and Archaic hunter-gatherers knew this region many thousand of years ago, but real settlement did not begin until after A.D. 400, as evidenced by pithouse villages downriver from El Morro, near Zuni. In the mid-1200s, Pueblo Indians in the Zuni area, apparently coping with drought conditions, decided to move to the higher elevation of El Morro, where they knew that the increased precipitation would benefit farming.

The settlers established seven communities in the valley, each consisting of up to thirty separate small housing clusters. In each, at least one site

was situated on a high point with a view over the valley, whose overall population attained several thousand people. These communities, however, were short-lived, for between A.D. 1275 and 1300, their inhabitants left to build larger consolidated pueblos like Atsinna on top of the mesas.

Atsinna has more than five hundred rooms arranged around an interior courtyard. From the walls, which had no exterior entrances, sentries could survey the entire valley. This defensive design suggests that Atsinna may have been threatened by its neighbors. Why? Archaeology does not tell, but one might speculate that in hard times villages were raiding each other for food stores.

While surveying the El Morro valley some years ago, archaeologist Steven LeBlanc found that a pueblo across the valley appeared to be an architectural blueprint of Atsinna. Each pueblo apparently was planned as a complete unit, constructed in a single building period, then occupied by its tenants, like an apartment complex today.

In the early 1300s, the residents of Atsinna and five other similar communities moved back downriver to the Zuni area. There they founded or resettled the six pueblos that Vasquez de Coronado encountered 250 years later. One was Hawikuh (p. 126), which the Spaniards stormed in 1640; another was Halona, whose remains still underlie the old part of present-day Zuni Pueblo.

A wing of Atsinna was excavated in the 1950s by archaeologist Richard B. Woodbury and was later stabilized by the Park Service. Woodbury reported that its inhabitants collected rainwater from natural rock basins and several small reservoirs on the mesa. Of course, the pool below provided water, too, though carrying it up the steep mesa trail would have been a tiresome chore.

The trail to Atsinna involves a short strenuous climb, but the view is worth the effort. You will see a dozen excavated masonry rooms and two kivas. The path continues across the mesa to a second undisturbed ruin, then descends the back side of the cliff and loops around to the starting place. You should allow about an hour and a half for the complete hike and more time to study the historic inscriptions.

El Morro is a particularly satisfying place to visit because it combines beautiful scenery with an interesting historical and cultural dimension. There is an attractive picnic area and a campground. You can obtain gas in Ramah, fifteen miles away, and you will find plenty of travel services in Grants and Gallup. As an adjunct to El Morro, you may wish to visit Zuni Pueblo or take a hike on the Zuni–Acoma Trail (p. 120) in nearby El Malpais National Monument.

Suggested reading: *Zuni and El Morro: Past and Present*, edited by David Grant Noble, Ancient City Press, Santa Fe, New Mexico, 1993.

*Atsinna Pueblo, El Morro National Monument.*

# Zuni Area Sites

*Zuni Pueblo is located along New Mexico 53, 35 miles south of Gallup, New Mexico. Zuni policy concerning access to Hawikuh and Village of the Great Kivas changes. To obtain permission, call (505) 782-4481; then call (505) 782-4814 for directions.*

At the time of the Spanish entrada in 1540, the Zunis were a prosperous nation numbering about three thousand people who inhabited six villages: Hawikuh, Matsaki, Kiakima, Kwakina, Kechipauan, and Halona. Halona is at the heart of present-day Zuni Pueblo. Archaeologists date the presence of Zuni culture in this area to the mid-1200s. Other Puebloan sites, including Village of the Great Kivas, however, have even greater antiquity. If you go to Zuni, you can stroll through the old part of the pueblo, visit the restored Our Lady of Guadeloupe church, have lunch in a local cafe, and shop for Zuni craft arts. Depending on current policy, you may also be able to visit Hawikuh and Village of the Great Kivas.

## Hawikuh

In 1540, Francisco Vasquez de Coronado led a Spanish expeditionary force to New Mexico and in mid-summer arrived at the the Zuni town of Hawikuh. When the Zunis denied his army access to the pueblo, his soldiers stormed and occupied the town and proceeded to use it as a base to further explore the American Southwest.

Today, Hawikuh consists of rubble-strewn mounds, but in 1540, it was a formidable, multistoried, hilltop town. As the Spanish soldiers approached it from a distance, their hopes regarding what was hidden within its walls probably ran high. After gaining entrance, however, their disappointment must have been all the more bitter. Hawikuh's substantial houses were made of stone and mortar, but its inhabitants owned none of what the Europeans deemed wealth. Still, as Coronado's chronicler later wrote, "We found what we needed more than gold and silver, and that was much corn, and beans and turkeys...." After their long, arduous trek and all-day battle, the conquistadores ate well and rested before detachments of soldiers were dispatched to explore the Rio Grande Valley, the land of the Hopis, and other parts of the Southwest

When the Spaniards later colonized New Mexico, Franciscan priests set out for the Zuni villages to preach the gospel and build churches at Hawikuh and Halona. Having a long-established religion of their own, the Indians did not welcome the missionaries and resisted their theology. Hawikuh's church was repeatedly burned, the last time being in 1680, when the Pueblo Indians rose up to overthrow Spanish rule. They also abandoned Hawikuh at this time and never returned.

*The mounds of Hawikuh.*

Archaeological excavations were carried out at Hawikuh by Frederick Webb Hodge in 1922 and 1923. Although he confirmed that the site was inhabited as early as A.D. 1300, he was primarily interested in the period of Spanish-Indian contact, and he left earlier (deeper) levels of the site for later researchers to probe. In Hodge's time, backfilling an excavation as a preservation method was not practiced, so weathering eventually reduced the exposed standing walls to rubble mounds.

> Suggested reading: *History of Hawikuh,* New Mexico: One of the So-called Cities of Cibola, by Frederick W. Hodge, Southwest Museum, Los Angeles, California, 1937.

## Village of the Great Kivas

Village of the Great Kivas had already long been abandoned when Coronado's army marched into New Mexico. The site is named for two large kivas that appear as circular depressions in front of the ruins. These consist mostly of mounds; however, a few of the pueblo's eighteen rooms are exposed. The banded masonry walls identify this site as an outlying great house of Chaco Canyon (p. 113), which is sixty miles to the northeast.

Village of the Great Kivas was excavated in the 1930s by Frank H. H. Roberts, Jr., an archaeologist best known for his research at Shabik'eshchee Village, a large Basketmaker site in Chaco Canyon.

*Zuni pictographs, Village of the Great Kivas.*

Roberts found that the pueblo dated to between A.D. 1000 and 1150, when Chaco was at its peak. After Chaco's collapse, the inhabitants of the village may have remained in this area, later to blend with the Zuni culture. They made numerous petroglyphs in the rocks above the site. In the early or mid-twentieth century, Zuni Indians painted two panels of figures and masks in a sheltered alcove around the mesa.

At Zuni Pueblo, you will find gas stations, cafes, craft shops, and a campground. More travel services can be found in Gallup. Atsinna, another prehistoric Zuni site, can be visited at nearby El Morro National Monument (p. 123). Casamero Pueblo (p. 117) is another Chacoan great house site, located off Interstate 40 between Grants and Gallup.

> Suggested reading: "Village of the Great Kivas on the Zuni Reservation, New Mexico," by Frank H. H. Roberts, Jr., *Bureau of American Ethnology Bulletin 111*, 1932.

## Aztec Ruins National Monument

*Aztec Ruins National Monument is located on Ruins Road, one-half mile north of U.S. 550 on the north side of Aztec, New Mexico, about 14 miles north of Farmington. Information: (505) 334-6174. Entrance fee.*

In 1947, a resident of the Aztec area recollected his experiences exploring Aztec Ruins nearly seventy years earlier.

We broke a hole through the wall and entered the room to the northeast, and there we really did see things! I got into that room and stood, trying my best to take it all in and see everything I could, while that excited crowd were rummaging it, scattering and turning everything into a mess. There were thirteen skeletons ranging from infants to adults....There were several baskets, some of the best that I have ever seen, all well preserved. There were a lot of sandals, some very good, others showing considerable wear. There

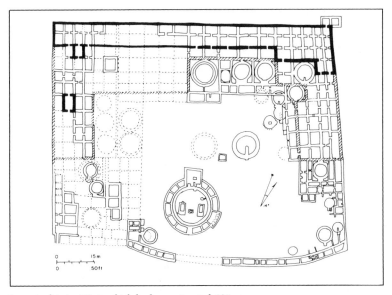

*Layout of Aztec West, which had an estimated 405 rooms and 28 kivas. Courtesy National Park Service.*

was a large quantity of pottery....There were a great many beads and ornaments...[and] quite a lot of turquoise.

When we had finished this work, the stuff was taken out and carried off by different members of the party, but where is it now? Nobody knows....it is gone. I, being only a small kid, did not get my choice of artifacts. I had to take what was left, which made a nice little collection, at that. But it, too, is about all gone.

Sealed tombs and buried treasure contain a romance and mystery that has lit a fire under both pothunters and archaeologists. Earl H. Morris, who devoted much of his professional life to excavating and restoring this ancient site along the Animas River, remembered digging up his first pot at age three and a half, "the clinching event that was to make me an ardent pot hunter, who, later on was to acquire the more creditable, and I hope earned, classification as an archaeologist."

By the time Morris began his investigations in Aztec's West Ruin in 1916 under the auspices of the American Museum of Natural History, parts of the site had been repeatedly looted, its artifacts given away, lost, sold, or destroyed. But this large ancient pueblo still contained a trove of cultural material, much of it in the lower-story rooms, which were well sealed off from the ravages of looters and weather.

Morris noticed that artifacts uncovered in Aztec's earliest components were Chacoan in style and those of the pueblo's last occupation were Mesa Verdean. Between, he recorded a thin layer of what archaeologists term "sterile fill" (windblown dirt containing no cultural material),

*Well-preserved ceiling in Aztec Room.*

which represented a period of vacancy. He deduced, therefore, that the town had originally been built by Chacoan Anasazi people, then briefly abandoned, and finally reoccupied by Mesa Verdean Anasazi. Subsequent tree research has placed the Chacoans at Aztec from A.D. 1110 to 1275. One Chaco scholar, Stephan H. Lekson, believes Aztec's Chacoan ruling class moved south to establish a new power base at Paquimé (p. 27). Ordinary Anasazi farmers lived continuously in the Animas–San Juan region before and briefly after activity at Aztec.

Some of Earl Morris's findings in Aztec West were truly spectacular. In one partially burned room in the east wing, he excavated tens of thousands of shell beads, hundreds of quartzite arrowheads, mosaic pendants of abalone shell, a seventy-five-foot necklace made up of 40,000 beads, 200 bushels of charred corn, and quantities of pottery vessels and effigies.

Another rare find was the burial of a six-foot-two-inch man interred with jewelry and wrapped in a turkey-feather blanket. He had with him a large decorated basketry shield, numerous bowls and jars, objects believed to be wooden swords, and other items.

When you visit Aztec, you will want to take a tour of the west wing, where you can explore a series of well-preserved rooms demonstrating fine masonry workmanship. Also be sure to enter Aztec's reconstructed great kiva with its massive columns and roof beams. Within this impressive subterranean room, you can try to imagine Anasazi ceremonial life centuries ago.

Impressive as the ruins of Aztec West are, it is important to realize that this excavated building was part of a much larger local community. Aztec East, within the national monument has long been known. In the 1980s, archaeologists found many nearby Puebloan sites along the river terrace west and north of the national monument boundaries. Within a two-mile stretch, they recorded the remains of thirty-seven Anasazi residential buildings, seven great houses, thirteen great kivas, three road systems, numerous earthworks, and a couple of quarries. The largest of the buildings has an estimated 110 rooms.

The Aztec community was built intensively at the same time that Chaco Canyon was being abandoned and the prehistoric Great North Road seems to connect the two centers. Given these factors, it is no wonder that many scholars now call Aztec "the new Chaco."

Aztec Ruins is a large, well-preserved, carefully interpreted, and easily accessible site with a good museum. It you are interested in Southwestern prehistory, be sure to include it in your itinerary. From here you can conveniently make trips to Salmon Ruins (below), which is only twelve miles away, and Chaco Canyon (p. 113).

Suggested reading: *Earl Morris & Southwestern Archaeology,* by Florence C. Lister and Robert H. Lister, University of New Mexico Press, Albuquerque, New Mexico, 1968. *Aztec Ruins on the Animas,* by Robert H. Lister and Florence C. Lister, University of New Mexico Press, 1987.

# Salmon Ruins

*The Salmon Ruins and museum are located at 975 U.S. Highway 64 between Bloomfield and Farmington, New Mexico. Information: (505) 632-2013. Entrance fee.*

The Salmon Ruins is a three hundred-room pueblo situated on an alluvial terrace above the floodplain of the San Juan River. This river originates in the San Juan Mountains of the southern Rockies and drains a large portion of the Southwest before flowing into Lake Powell to mingle with the waters of the Colorado River.

When you visit archaeological sites in the Four Corners region, you soon learn that the exodus of prehistoric Pueblo people from here coincided with a major drought between 1276 and 1299. This is part of the story of Salmon Pueblo. But wouldn't you think that in times of drought, people would gravitate *to* a major river like the San Juan, rather than *away from* it? The suggestion here is that other factors besides water scarcity were probably involved in Anasazi migrations of the late thirteenth century.

Like nearby Aztec Pueblo, Salmon's first inhabitants were Chacoan Anasazi, who settled here about A.D. 1088. They quarried sandstone to make building blocks for the pueblo's thick walls and may have floated pine logs down the San Juan River and its tributaries from the forested

*The remains of Salmon Pueblo.*

*Chaco masonry at Salmon Ruins.*

highlands of southwestern Colorado. Chimney Rock Pueblo (p. 135), near Pagosa Springs, has been cited as one potential source area. Salmon's architects built a pueblo according to the classic Chacoan great-house design. A prehistoric road probably linked their town to Chaco Canyon, fifty miles to the south.

Salmon's first occupants, however, did not stay long, scarcely two generations. After they left, their pueblo lay deserted for nearly a century and fell into disrepair. Then, between A.D. 1225 and 1240, several hundred Anasazi, probably from nearby communities along the river, reoccupied the pueblo. They renovated many rooms, added several kivas, and stayed for fifty or sixty years before they too left. Cynthia Irwin-Williams, the archaeologist who directed excavations of Salmon in the mid-1970s, commented that "the use of physical space was completely different in the two occupations. The Chacoans required—since they built them that way—large, light, airy, spacious quarters. The secondary occupants...did not need such quarters...possibly because they were used to living in smaller houses."

A tragic event occurred at Salmon Pueblo in the 1260s. As archaeologists reconstruct it, a fire broke out in the ceiling of a room and began to spread throughout the surrounding complex. Fifty young children, who apparently initially escaped the conflagration, were gathered for safety on a nearby kiva roof. When the roof collapsed, they fell inside where they perished in temperatures so hot that the sand on the floor was fused into glass. Prehistoric pueblos, with their wood roofs and compact quarters, could be veritable fire traps. Conflagrations such as happened at Salmon Pueblo, while seldom resulting in such horrific consequences, were not uncommon.

When you walk about this site and other Chacoan great houses, think about the labor and degree of architectural planning and engineering skills required in their construction. The Chaco Anasazi certainly had a dynamic and well-organized society, but for any society, no amount of social and political organization or military might can long endure a shortage of rainfall. When drought continues and appeals to the supernatural powers to send rain go unheeded, social turmoil and civil strife are certain to follow. This may explain the fate of Salmon Pueblo in the late 1200s.

In 1968, San Juan County purchased the Salmon site, thus saving it from being mined for antiquarian souvenirs. Subsequent funds to preserve and study the ruins were contributed by the State of New Mexico, the National Endowment for the Humanities, and other private sources.

You can stroll through the ruins using an interpretive self-guiding booklet. One impressive feature to note within the apartment complex is a tower kiva built of specially selected stone on a twenty-foot platform. Be sure also to spend time in the museum and tour the rustic homestead of the Salmon family, who were Mormon pioneers in this area. You will find many travel services in the Farmington area. From the Salmon Ruins, it is but a short drive to Aztec Ruins National Monument (p.128).

Suggested reading: *The Chacoan Prehistory of the San Juan Basin,* by R. Gwinn Vivian, Academic Press, San Diego, California, 1990.

# Chimney Rock Archaeological Area

*The Chimney Rock Archaeological Area is located along Colorado 151, 3 miles south of its intersection with U.S. 160, which is 20 miles west of Pagosa Springs. Scheduled guided tours of this group of sites are conducted daily between May 15 and September 30. The tour takes two and a half hours. Reservations are needed for groups of ten or more. Information: Pagosa Springs Ranger District, San Juan National Forest, P.O. Box 310, Pagosa Springs, CO 81147, (970) 264-2268 or (970) 264-2268. Entrance fee.*

With its commanding view over the western foothills of the southern Rockies and the Rio Piedra, Chimney Rock Pueblo is special among archaeological sites. It lies in the shadow of a dramatic pinnacle, Chimney Rock, which was a familiar landmark to Indians, pioneers, and fur trappers, and presently serves as an aerie for peregrine falcons.

Archaeological surveys in this general area have turned up hundreds of sites spanning a long time period. The best known among them is Chimney Rock Pueblo, a remote Chacoan outlier built in the late eleventh century.

The Chimney Rock district must have been known to Basketmaker people long before the Anasazi pueblo builders arrived here in the late

800s or early 900s. Archaeologists have recorded Basketmaker dwellings and pithouse settlements near the floodplains of streams along the Colorado–New Mexico border and in the region now submerged under the waters of Navajo Reservoir. These early folk experimented with growing domesticated plants and learned the craft of pottery making and how to hunt with the bow and arrow.

Anasazi–Pueblo people—those who built above-ground masonry houses and villages—lived on the mesas and along the canyons of these foothills for at least two hundred years before the building of Chimney Rock Pueblo. Probably migrating up the Rio Piedra drainage from the San Juan River in the tenth century, they were the true pioneers of this rugged high country, whose short growing season made maize farming tenuous at best.

These backcountry folk built isolated dwellings and small hamlets on the lower mesas. While they did tend garden plots of corn and beans in places near water, hunting large game such as deer and elk remained an important part of their economy, as did foraging for wild plants. They had two other resources, too: timber for building and trading, and river water to transport logs to the lowlands, the heartland of Anasazi culture. What is remarkable about the inhabitants of Chimney Rock was their ability to cope with high-altitude subsistence, including long winters of bitter cold and deep snows.

The real highlight of your visit here is seeing Chimney Rock Pueblo, a Chacoan great house. It is situated at an elevation of 7,600 feet on a narrow triangular mesa, which is attained by climbing a steep slope and crossing a causeway, each side of which falls precipitously for hundreds of feet. From their high perch, the Chacoan occupants of the great house gazed down on a surrounding community of Mesa Verdean farmers. If you hike up to the site, you will be rewarded by a breathtaking view of the wooded hills and canyons, not to mention the twin spires of Chimney Rock and its mate, Companion Rock.

The Chacoans built, or more likely supervised the construction of, this two-story pueblo in the 1090s. They must have impressed the locals and recruited them to contribute the labor to built this fifty-five-room, high-flying building. The pueblo is Chacoan through and through. It was a preplanned structure. Its core-and-veneer masonry walls, neatly laid up with layered and chinked sandstone blocks, show the engineering and design skills the Chacoan craftsmen are known for. The compact architecture and spacious rooms, which enclose two kivas, also signals Chaco's influence.

There is no water on this little mesa, which is twelve hundred feet above the river, and only bedrock to build on. So envision the construction site: Just to make building mortar, teams of laborers had to haul dirt and water up here (probably using pitch-coated wicker bas-

*View of Chimney Rock and Companion Rock from the ruins.*

*Chimnney Rock Pueblo and view over the Rio Piedra Valley.*

kets) from far below, a laborious task, indeed. And why bother? This is probably the single most compelling question in the field of Southwestern archaeology today. Clearly, the Chacoans had great influence, but upon what was it based? Were they conquerors, colonists, traders, or missionaries? A glance at Western history suggests they might have been all these together.

Archaeologists have asked what attracted the sophisticated Chacoans to this hinterland, whose inhabitants must have seemed very backward. One theory, called the lumber camp model, suggests it was timber. The Chacoans needed timber to build Pueblo Bonito, Chetro Ketl, and the rest of their monumental buildings in Chaco Canyon. It is estimated they used two hundred thousand logs just for roof timbers in these structures. Here is how the lumber camp advocates say it might have worked. By using military might or the inspirational power of religion, the Chacoans recruited local laborers to build their "castle" and develop a timber industry. The workers would girdle trees and leave them to die and dry out for a couple of years. Then they would fell them with stone axes, skid the logs down the hillsides in winter, and float them down the Piedra and San Juan in the spring floods. At some point downriver, perhaps at Salmon Pueblo (p. 132), the logs would be pulled ashore and carried to Chaco Canyon. Is it not a credible hypothesis? If and when trace-mineral analyses of Chaco's existing roof beams are done, the theory stands to be verified or dismissed.

Southwestern Indians place much cultural significance on the believed connections between particular landscape features and their historical/religious narratives. Some scholars have speculated that the Indians saw the two pinnacles as manifestations of the Twin War Gods, who are so important in Pueblo mythology. Did they build this great house as a shrine to these mythic heros?

Still another avenue of research is based on astronomy. In 1988, an archaeoastronomy study here revealed an interesting phenomenon. As J. McKim Malville and Claudia Putnam describe it in their book, *Prehistoric Astronomy in the Southwest,* "We discovered that the moon would rise in the gap between the pinnacles, near the time of the major northern standstill.... For periods of little more than two years each 18.6-year period, the moon reaches a sufficiently high northern declination to rise between the pinnacles as seen by watchers near the Chimney Rock Pueblo." There is no question, Chimney Rock Pueblo is a truly fascinating site whose significance touches many dimensions.

Archaeological studies in the Chimney Rock district began in 1921 with surveys and excavations by J. A. Jeancon and Frank H. H. Roberts, Jr., sponsored by the Colorado State Historical Society and other organizations. Between 1970 and 1972, more work was done here by Frank W. Eddy of the University of Colorado. He recorded more than ninety sites and excavated four to prepare for public tours.

After arriving at the entrance gate to Chimney Rock, you will follow your guide by car to the parking area where the walking tour begins. Along the first (easy part) of the trail, you will pass an excavated great kiva, numerous small pueblo structures, three large circular rooms, and an unusual circular hole carefully hand-carved into the bedrock. The most challenging part of the tour is walking up to Chimney Rock Pueblo. Do not be put off by the five hundred-foot ascent, for it leads to a memorable reward. Along the trail you will traverse the causeway, pass the "guardhouse" (a series of rooms perched on the cliff's edge), and finally arrive at the impressive great house on top with its view of the countryside. Bring a water bottle and binoculars.

You will find plenty of accomodations and travel services in Durango and Pagosa Springs. Chimney Rock is an isolated site, but with a little driving, you can reach Mesa Verde (p. 55), Aztec Ruins (p. 128), and even Chaco Canyon.

Suggested reading: *In the Shadow of the Rocks: Archaeology of the Chimney Rock District in Southern Colorado,* by Florence C. Lister, The Durango Herald, Durango, Colorado, 1997.

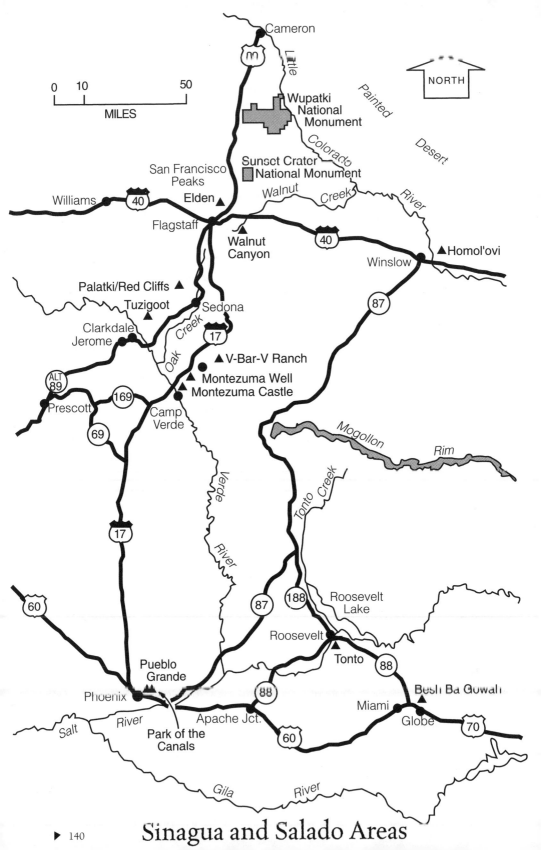

NORTH

Cameron

Little

Painted

Wupatki
National
Monument

Colorado

Desert

0   10        50
MILES

Sunset Crater
National Monument

River

San Francisco
Peaks

Walnut        Creek

Williams    40    Elden ▲
Flagstaff                    40

▲ Homol'ovi

Walnut
Canyon                         Winslow

Palatki/Red Cliffs ▲

87

Tuzigoot
▲

Sedona

Clarkdale             17
Jerome

Oak  Creek

▲V-Bar-V Ranch

ALT
89                169

▲
Montezuma Well
Montezuma Castle

Mogollon        Rim

Prescott

Camp
Verde

69

Verde

Tonto  Creek

17

River

60

87   188   Roosevelt
Lake

Pueblo
Grande

Roosevelt
▲
Tonto       88

Besh Ba Gowah
▲

Phoenix

88

Miami

Globe       70

Salt    River    Apache Jct.

Park of the
Canals

60

Gila    River

▶ 140

# Sinagua and Salado Areas

# The Sinagua and the Salado
## People in Between

The Sinagua and the Salado are two little-known cultures of the Southwest whose remains are found in central and northern Arizona. Both groups were strongly influenced by their surrounding Mogollon, Anasazi, and Hohokam neighbors. Eventually, they blended with these groups, thus disappearing from the archaeological record.

### The Sinagua

Despite their name, which means "without water" in Spanish, the Sinagua (seen-awa) did have water and were successful farmers in the region between the San Francisco Peaks, near Flagstaff, Arizona, and the Verde Valley to the south.

Around A.D. 675, early Sinagua Indians made their homes in rustic pithouses on the mountain slopes where the piñon-juniper uplands meet the higher-elevation ponderosa forests. They used both zones for hunting and gathering and raised crops in the fertile alluvial soils of basins along the flanks of the mountains. Initially small in population, their numbers grew, and by A.D. 900, they had established active trading relations with Kayenta Anasazi people to the north and Hohokam communities to the south. Their farming methods also became more sophisticated, as evidenced today by the remains of terraces and field houses.

The southern Sinagua farmed the fertile mesas along the Mogollon Rim, using rocks as a garden mulch to moderate soil temperatures and lengthen the growing season. They exchanged goods with the Hohokam, who apparently taught them irrigation technology and introduced them to the ballcourt (p. 34).

*Imported pottery excavated at Elden Pueblo.*

Travelers approaching Flagstaff today from the north or east will notice the presence of a number of cinder cones. In 1064, a series of volcanic eruptions began, forming Sunset Crater and spreading an estimated half-billion tons of cinders and ash over some eight hundred square miles. Off and on for two centuries, the eruptions continued to produce ash, cinders, and lava flows. These momentous events must have profoundly affected the lives of local residents. For a glimpse into this geologic history, you will find a visit to Sunset Crater National Monument most rewarding.

Archaeologists have long pondered what impact Sunset Crater's eruptions had on the Sinagua. An obvious research difficulty lies in the fact that many pre-eruptive archaeological sites remain buried beneath layers of cinders and ash. Theories about Sinagua prehistory have changed as scientific knowledge has become more refined about when the eruptions occurred and what impact they had on the local ecology, agricultural practices, and population movements.

After about A.D. 1150, the northern Sinagua reached their highest cultural expression (Elden Phase), which is apparent in technological achievements such as monumental architecture, more complex social organization, and a marked growth in population. Large villages, such as Elden Pueblo (p.145) and Ridge Ruin, were established, and Sinagua settlements spread into the Wupatki and Walnut Canyon areas (pp. 148, and 151, respectively) and as far away as the Mogollon Rim.

The discovery of the Magician's Burial at Ridge Ruin offers a clue to possible social stratification. The contents of this grave, which included more than six hundred objects of pottery, basketry, turquoise and shell jewelry, arrows, wooden wands, and a turquoise-inlaid nose plug, certainly indicate it contained someone of high elite status. Hopi Indians who have studied these burial goods recognize this person as having been a high-ranking member of their Motswimi or Warrior Society.

*Wupatki Pueblo.*

Their belief that some Hopi clans have Sinagua ancestry is supported by archaeological data.

Developments among the southern Sinagua parallel those of the Flagstaff area. They had settled the Verde Valley by around A.D. 700. This well-watered valley, which lies four thousand feet lower in elevation than Flagstaff, offered an ideal environment for foraging, farming, and living. Construction at Tuzigoot (p. 163), Montezuma Castle (p. 159), Palatki (p. 153), and many other communities in the Verde Valley did not begin until the mid-1200s. By 1300, many of the southern Sinagua people had concentrated in large visible sites, such as Tuzigoot and Montezuma Castle, that dominated smaller, satellite pueblos.

The northern Sinagua left many of the villages around the San Francisco Peaks in the late 1200s and the 1300s to move southeast to sites such as Nuvakwewtaqa on Anderson Mesa and to the Verde Valley. A century or so later, the southern Sinagua packed up and departed from the Verde Valley, also headed to Anderson Mesa.

At this point, Sinagua culture begins to blend with that of the Hopi, who view the Anderson Mesa sites as ancestral. The Hopi have legends regarding their heritage in Sinagua country: Sunset Crater is the abode of the wind god, Yaponcha; the Kachinas, their supernatural friends, make their home in the San Francisco Peaks; and the moisture-laden clouds, which rise over those mountains in summer and drift over the Hopi mesas to drop rain, embody the spirits of their ancestors.

Suggested reading: *The Sinagua,* by Rose Houk, Southwest Parks and Monuments Association, Tucson, Arizona, 1992.

## The Salado

Archaeologists are at odds about the Salado, not even agreeing that a distinct and separate Salado culture existed. To determine if a prehistoric culture existed, scholars traditionally turn to its "trait list," a list of distinctive artifacts found in a given region in a given time period. The longer the list, the more secure they feel in assigning the culture its own name. The problem with the Salado, as one scholar has written, is that "...sites labeled Salado are considered as such generally on the basis of the presence of Salado polychrome [pottery] alone."

Perhaps the best known Salado pottery is Gila polychrome, which was produced between the late 1200s and early 1400s. Noted for its black and white designs on a red base, it has been greatly acclaimed for its aesthetic qualities.

Quite apart from the validity of the term Salado, the people who made Salado polychrome certainly existed and surely had a name for themselves. They lived in the Tonto Basin and Globe-Miami area in Arizona, built pueblos and cliff dwellings, practiced agriculture, manufactured a variety of craft arts, and behaved in ways quite similar to those of their Mogollon, Hohokam, and Anasazi neighbors.

It was the legendary explorer-anthropologist Adolph F. Bandelier, after whom a national monument is named (p. 197), who first noted Salado sites around Globe in 1883, a very early date in southwestern archaeological history. He was followed in the 1920s by Erich F. Schmidt from the American Museum of Natural History. Schmidt excavated numerous sites and created a significant Salado database. Also in the 1920s, Harold and Winifred Gladwin established a major research center knows as

*Gila polychrome pot. Courtesy Office of Archaeological Studies, Museum of New Mexico. Photo by Nancy Warren.*

Gila Pueblo in Globe, which focused on Salado studies.

Gila Polychrome ceramics begins to disappear from the archaeological record in the early fifteenth century and 1450 is usually cited as the terminal date for the culture. The Salado people moved on to greener pastures. Unfortunately, the Salado sites of the Tonto Basin were inundated after Roosevelt Dam was completed in 1911. Since the science of archaeology was still in its infancy then, many questions concerning the culture will not be definitively answered. The only Salado sites that are open to the public are two cliff dwellings in Tonto National Monument (p. 167) and Besh Ba Gowah Pueblo (p. 168) in Globe.

Suggested reading: "The 1976 Salado Conference," edited by David E. Doyel and Emil W. Haury, *The Kiva*, vol. 42, no. 1, The Arizona Archaeological and Historical Society, Tucson, Arizona, 1976.

# Elden Pueblo

*Elden Pueblo is on the west side of U.S. 89, 1.8 miles north of this highway's interchange with Interstate 40, in Flagstaff, Arizona. Information: (520) 527-3600.*

Elden Pueblo, an important northern-Sinagua site on the outskirts of Flagstaff, has been the subject of a relatively new type of research known as public or participatory archaeology. Organized groups of students, be they school children or Elderhostel members, come to Elden to learn about the past by participating in the archaeological process. Under the supervision of a professional archaeologist, they methodically excavate portions of the site and record their findings.

The program has helped to dispel the exclusivity of traditional archaeology and introduce a broad spectrum of people to the value and fascination of studying past cultures. It also has contributed to the transformation of Elden Pueblo from a cluster of half-forgotten mounds to an educational park. Elden Pueblo's public program has been developed and administered by Coconino National Forest archaeologists with support from other organizations. (For further information, write to The Elden Pueblo Project, Arizona Natural History Association, P.O. Box 3496, Flagstaff, Arizona 86003.)

This sixty-five-room pueblo thrived between about A.D. 1150 and 1275 in a shady ponderosa forest at the base of Mount Elden. Rocks eroding from the mountain provided building stones used by Elden's residents, and a spring on its slopes offered at least one permanent water source. Only a few miles to the northeast is Sunset Crater (now a national monument), whose eruptions, beginning in A.D. 1064, transformed the environment of the Flagstaff area. Elden's inhabitants were blessed with a rich and varied environment in which they could gather many native plants for food and medicine and hunt game, including elk, deer, antelope, mountain sheep, bear, squirrels, gophers, rabbits, and turkeys. They also planted crops in alluvial parks within half a mile of their home.

All indications are that Elden Pueblo was a significant regional center in the twelfth and thirteenth centuries. In addition to farmers and crafts people, archaeologists believe its population included some individuals of high hereditary rank. The Hopi Indians, who call the site Pasiwvi, "place of coming together," view Elden as the former home of members of their Snake, Water, Badger, Antelope, and other clans. As recently as the 1930, Hopis stopped at Elden to pray while traveling to the San Francisco Peaks, their sacred mountains. Hopi oral history regarding Elden Pueblo reinforces archaeologists' views that the Sinagua people played a role in the development of Hopi culture.

Elden Pueblo was partially excavated in 1926 by two well-known figures in Southwestern anthropology: Jesse Walter Fewkes and John Peabody Harrington of the Smithsonian Institution. From 1966 to 1968, Roger E. Kelly directed a Northern Arizona University field school at this site. This pueblo, which is the type site for the Elden Phase of Sinagua culture, still holds promise for continuing archaeological study.

When you visit Elden Pueblo, pick up a copy of the trail guide and follow the interpretive path around the site. The first feature you will see is the "community room," which measures thirty by thirty-six feet. Four times larger than the pueblo's typical residential and storage rooms, it is encircled by a bench. Its floor was covered by many layers of mud plaster, and a slab-lined ventilator shaft allowed fresh air to enter the space. Probably it was used as a meeting room for all the pueblo's residents.

*Reconstruction at Elden Pueblo. Illustration by Brian Donahue.*
*Courtesy Coconino National Forest.*

*Along the interpretive trail at Elden Pueblo.*

Elden has some other interesting features. It is surrounded on at least three sides by the remains of formalized activity areas with plastered surfaces and storage and roasting pits. Also, three cemeteries lie just outside the main building complex. Along the trail, you will see a kiva, the walls of excavated rooms, and a plaza area.

While you are in the Flagstaff area, make time to visit the Museum of Northern Arizona, where you will find exhibits relating to this region's cultural history. Visits to nearby Wupatki and Walnut Canyon national monuments (pp. 148 and 151, respectively) are also recommended.

Suggested reading: "The Destruction of Elden Pueblo: A Hopi Story," by Edmund Nequatewa, in *Plateau,* no. 28, vol. 2, Museum of Northern Arizona, Flagstaff, Arizona, 1955.

*Wukoki Pueblo, Wupatki National Monument.*

# Wupatki National Monument

*Wupatki National Monument is 14 miles east of Arizona 89 between Flagstaff and Cameron. A 36-mile driving loop from Arizona 89 passes through this monument and Sunset Crater National Monument. Information: (520) 679-2365. Entrance fee.*

Wupatki National Monument, where the ruins of Wupatki, Wukoki, Citadel, Lomaki, and other sites are to be found, is marked by one of the most spacious and desolate panoramas in the Southwest. Temperatures here can plummet to zero in winter and rise to above 110 degrees in summer. The area's scant rains evaporate quickly in the dry heat and sweeping winds. Life forms must be hardy indeed to survive such extremes. This desert seems an unlikely locale to have sustained a human population that once reached several thousand people.

The finding of an eleven-thousand-year-old Clovis spear point (p. 2) suggests that some of the Southwest's first human residents roamed through the Wupatki area. Along the gravel terraces of the Little Colorado River, archaeologists also have found stone-tool manufacturing sites used by Archaic people prior to A.D. 500.

Today, the cinders deposited by a sequence of eruptions of Sunset Crater, which began in A.D. 1064, are still much in evidence. However,

*Petroglyphs at Wupatki National Monument.*

the fact that so many Sinagua Indian homes were deeply buried has made it difficult to estimate the area's early population. Researchers have speculated on the effects that such cinder and ash deposits might have had on agriculture: Where not too deep and after some decomposition had occurred, they probably acted as a moisture-conserving mulch and benefitted farming.

The population of the Wupatki area increased in the mid-1100s—a period of unusually high rainfall—and many Kayenta Anasazi people moved into the area to build highly visible masonry pueblos such as Wukoki, Citadel, and Lomaki. The densest concentration of people was on Antelope Prairie in the western sector of the monument. This higher elevation offered farmers more precipitation with which to grow crops. They stayed in small field houses near their fields and built check dams to direct water flow to their garden plots.

A 1980s archaeological survey in the monument recorded some three thousand sites that showed a mix of prehistoric cultures were present in the area. In addition to the Sinagua, there were Kayenta Anasazi people, who came from the north; Winslow Anasazi from the east; Cohonina folk from the west; and even Hohokam, whose homeland was in the Phoenix Basin far to the south.

When you register at the visitor center, you will see Wupatki Pueblo, which was excavated in the 1930s. Tree-ring samples show this site to have been inhabited between about 1106 and 1225. It was occupied by Sinagua people. Found among these ruins were pieces of turquoise and shell jewelry, copper bells, textiles and baskets, cotton cloth, and scarlet macaw burials. Clearly, the occupants of Wupatki were involved in far-reaching trade. The presence of a Hohokam-style ball court near Wupatki Pueblo (p. 148)—the northernmost example of this type of structure—further underscores the influence of distant cultures upon this area. Scholars believe that ritual contests of religious and sportive significance were held here. Another nearby structure you will see is a large circular amphitheater, which may have served as a gathering place for the populace.

A driving loop through the monument leads to other ruins—Wukoki, Citadel, and Lomaki. The monument also has several fine petroglyph sites, especially in the vicinity of Crack-in-Rock ruins. (Check with the Park Service about access.) The glyphs depict humans playing flutes, hunting, and giving birth, and show a variety of animals, birds, and insects. Graphic designs are represented, too, including large spirals, which some Hopi and Zuni Indians say represent migrations. Many of Wupatki's petroglyph designs closely resemble motifs found on Flagstaff Black-on-white and Wupatki Black-on-white pottery, which date to between A.D. 1100 and 1225. Other glyph designs are similar to patterns on textiles dating between 1100 and 1300. Such a clear relationship between rock art, ceramic, and textile designs is unusual.

The historical period at Wupatki has witnessed an interesting series of developments. The stories of Navajo sheepherders, Mormon settlers, Anglo cattle ranchers, miners, traders, and railroad people calls for an entire book. One Navajo family, the descendants of Peshlakai Etsidi who moved here in 1870 after the Navajos' internment at Fort Sumner, still lives within the monument boundaries.

Wupatki's visitor center has exhibits on the region's cultural history. Although picnic sites are available, blustery winds in this area often discourage sitting outdoors. A visit to Sunset Crater will nicely compliment your experience of the Wupatki ruins, and a tour of Walnut Canyon National Monument (p. 151) will give you another perspective on the Sinagua culture. The city of Flagstaff has many travel services.

Suggested reading: *Letters from Wupatki,* by Courtney Reeder Jones, The University of Arizona Press, Tucson, Arizona, 1995.

*Cliff dwelling in Walnut Canyon.*

# Walnut Canyon National Monument

*Walnut Canyon National Monument is 3 miles from the Walnut Canyon exit (no. 204) on Interstate 40, 7 miles east of Flagstaff, Arizona. Information: (520) 526-3367. Entrance fee.*

Quite apart from archaeological considerations, a visit to Walnut Canyon is a memorable experience. Deeply cut through layers of limestone laid down on ancient seabeds, the canyon is a peaceful place whose quietude is broken only by the calls of birds and the sound of wind in the pines.

Almost as a bonus, Walnut Canyon has a good deal of archaeological and historical interest, for Sinagua Indians once lived here and before them hunter-gatherers knew the place. The canyon hummed with life between around A.D. 1150 and 1225. Some inhabitants lived in small pueblos along the rims, where they farmed, hunted, and gathered pine nuts. Near their dwellings, a number of unusual structures have been found with defensive, almost fort-like, attributes. As at Hovenweep (p. 67), researchers here have wondered if they were true forts, or if perhaps they housed visiting dignitaries, such as wealthy traders from Hohokam centers to the south.

Many Sinagua Indians chose to live within the canyon, building cliff dwellings in shallow caves eroded in the limestone cliffs. These are not the large pueblo complexes of Mesa Verde; rather, they are cozy extended-family dwellings scattered within earshot of each other throughout the area. The canyon's environment is highly varied, depending on elevation and exposure to direct sun—ponderosa pines can grow near cacti—and many plants are harvestable through the seasons of the year. There was good hunting, too, including deer and wild turkeys, both of which are still present in the area.

The Sinagua left Walnut Canyon in the mid-1200s, many traveling south to the Verde Valley, others drifting eastward toward present-day Winslow and the Hopi country. It is not well understood why they left their canyon homes. Puebloan people were not nomadic, but they did relocate quite regularly. One reason to move was depleted natural resources: When soils become spent, game disappears, and firewood grows scarce, it's time to move on.

After the coming of the railroad, European-Americans began to settle the Flagstaff area in growing numbers, and recreational outings to Walnut Canyon became a popular pastime. In the 1880s, this was a favorite place for pothunting. To facilitate digging in dark inner rooms, some looters went so far as to dynamite outer pueblo walls. Needless to say, such activities took a heavy toll on the cliff dwellings and their precious contents.

By the early 1900s, civic leaders in the town of Flagstaff realized that they were fast losing a potentially valuable tourist attraction and took measures to safeguard the ruins. Then, in 1915, President Woodrow Wilson named Walnut Canyon a national monument. Even so, it took nearly two more decades before adequate supervision of the archaeological sites was implemented. Depression-era programs like the Civilian Conservation Corps contributed to stabilizing the cliff dwellings, improving trails, and assigning guides to visitor groups.

Walnut Canyon's cliff dwellings had been so devastated by looters over the years that one archaeologist referred to the place as "a monument to vandalism." But the cliff houses, which had borne the brunt of the damages, were only one dimension of the area's archaeology; virtually untouched were other types of sites, especially on the rims, and researchers have found much to study in them.

The first among these researchers was Dr. Harold S. Colton, a zoology professor at the University of Pennsylvania. After Colton's initial visit to the canyon in 1912, he returned annually to study the ruins and survey the canyon. In 1926, he moved to Flagstaff with his family and founded the Museum of Northern Arizona. Colton was soon joined by Lyndon Hargrave, and together, they conducted the first professional excavation in the canyon. Archaeological research has continued sporadically over the decades. A complete monument survey in the 1980s recorded 242 sites ranging from small artifact scatters to multiroom pueblos.

There are two hiking trails in the monument. The Rim Trail begins at the parking lot, passes pueblo ruins and a pithouse, and continues to canyon overlooks. It is a flat 25-minute walk. The mile-long Island Trail, which has some up-and-down terrain, passes a series of the cliff dwellings and spectacular views. Bring your camera and binoculars.

As a jumping-off place for the Grand Canyon, Flagstaff has an abundance of travel services. You may wish to visit Elden Pueblo (p. 145) and the Museum of Northern Arizona while you are here, and take a drive through Oak Creek Canyon to Sedona.

Suggested reading: *Walnut Canyon National Monument,* by Scott Thybony, Southwest Parks and Monuments Association, Tucson, Arizona, 1996.

## Palatki, Red Cliffs, and Honanki

*Palatki and Red Cliffs are a 30-minute drive west of Sedona, Arizona. From Sedona, take Arizona 89A west for 7 miles to FR 525. Follow FR 525 north for 6 miles, then continue another 2 miles to Palatki and Red Cliffs. From there you can obtain directions to Honanki. Information: (520) 282-4119. Entrance fee.*

Sedona, Arizona, which is famous for its red rock landscapes, is located near numerous southern Sinagua ruins and rock art sites. Recently opened to the public by the U.S. Forest Service are two cliff dwellings and several interesting rock art panels. You can reach them on your own or by joining a guided jeep tour in town.

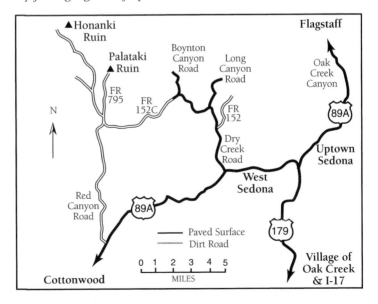

*Map showing roads to Palatki, Red Cliffs, and Honanki.*

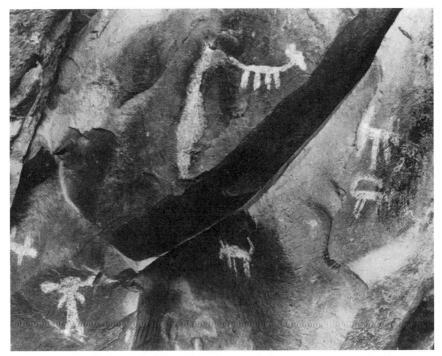

*Pictographs at Red Cliffs Rock Art Site at Palatki.*

In 1895, the archaeologist Jesse Walter Fewkes explored parts of Arizona and reported on the sites of Palatki, Red Cliffs, and Honanki. The name Palatki means "red house" in the Hopi language. Fewkes had become interested in the history and culture of the Hopi Indians. Hopi guides brought him here and to some of their other ancestral homes in the Verde Valley.

A short trail leads from Palatki's parking area to the ruins, which consist of two large dwellings built at the base of a sheer cliff in a box canyon. They were inhabited by Sinagua Indians for about two hundred years after A.D. 1100. The first pueblo, which you can walk around and enter, has impressively high walls made of red sandstone blocks. Some room walls are rounded, which is unusual and enhanced the structure's strength and durability. A white shield-like pictograph, visible high on the cliff face above the dwelling, is thought to be a clan symbol of the former residents. From this site, you can look west along the cliff to the remains of a second complex of masonry rooms, which are too deteriorated to allow closer access.

Another short trail leads to Red Cliffs, a series of alcoves containing panels of pictographs and petroglyphs. In the Grotto Alcove, the first one along the trail, you will find numerous abstract pictograph

*Palatki Ruin.*

designs—rakes, squiggly lines, and rows of dots—dating from the Archaic period (6,000 B.C. to A.D. 600). There are also pictures from the Sinagua period (A.D. 650 to 1400), some probably having been made by the residents of nearby Palatki.

The Bear Alcove has examples of Apache and Yavapai rock art, including bears, deer, and horseback riders. These tribes were living in the Verde Valley by the sixteenth century and were removed by the U.S. government in the late 1800s. In the Roasting Pit Alcove, you will see a large gray mound along the trail where Indians roasted agave hearts (a desert plant) for many generations. The walls of this alcove display a variety of rock art made over a long time period by different cultural groups.

Inquire at the Palatki-Red Cliffs ranger station for directions to Honanki, a large cliff dwelling site located several miles away. The road is rough in places. To reach Honanki involves about a ten-minute walk along an easy trail that then winds for a considerable distance along the base of a butte past a series of room remains and cave dwellings. You will also see examples of Archaic, Sinagua, Apache, and Yavapai rock art.

Honanki, or "Bear House," also was named by Fewkes when he was exploring the Verde Valley. The cliff dwelling, which dates to from A.D. 1130 to 1280, contained about sixty rooms and housed a substantial population. Today, the rooms are highly dilapidated due to erosion and vandalism. Honanki is the type site for the Honanki Phase (A.D. 1150–1300) of the southern Sinagua cultural sequence.

In his 1896 report to the Smithsonian Institution, Fewkes mentions many interesting artifacts that he found in Honanki's rooms. He seemed frustrated not to have the time and means to collect more than he did. His words, "I can readily predict a rich harvest for anyone who may attempt systematic work in this virgin field," reflect an outdated attitude toward professional archaeology and its purpose. From his findings, Fewkes deduced that Apache people reoccupied Honanki rooms (probably as camping sites) long after the Sinagua had departed.

While in this area, you should certainly plan to visit Tuzigoot and Montezuma Castle national monuments (pp. 163 and 159, respectively) and possibly the historic mining town of Jerome, as well. Many travel services are available in Sedona and Clarkdale.

Suggested reading: "The Pueblo III Period along the Mogollon Rim: the Honanki, Elden, and Turkey Hill Phases of the Sinagua," by Peter J. Pilles, Jr. in The Prehistoric Pueblo World: A.D. 1150–1350, edited by Michael A. Adler, University of Arizona Press, Tucson, Arizona, 1996.

# V-Bar-V Ranch Petroglyph Site

*The V-Bar-V Ranch Petroglyph Site is located 3.5 miles south of the intersection of Arizona 179 and Interstate 17, which is 12 miles south of Sedona, Arizona. Information: (520) 282-4119. Entrance fee.*

The V-Bar-V Ranch Petroglyph Site was only opened to the public in recent years, after the U.S. Forest Service acquired this ranch. Having been on private property for so long, the panel was spared the vandalism and defacement experienced by so many rock art sites in the Southwest. Today a professional site manager and stewards curate the site and serve as guides and interpreters when you visit.

The southern Sinagua people left rock art sites throughout the Verde Valley region, but many are not open to the public or easily accessible. With more than a thousand elements, the V-Bar-V site is the largest known single collection. You can walk right up to these glyphs (do not touch them), which are densely packed on a cliff surface. You may wonder who made all these pictures and for whom to see. The makers may have been residents of a Sinagua village whose ruins are located close by. And a trail along nearby Beaver Creek would have seen heavy traffic by local and regional travelers; from this trail, the petroglyphs were highly visible.

Other questions that come to mind are why they were made and what they mean. Here, the answers are more elusive. Rock art scholars theorize about meaning, and Native Americans—in this case, the Hopis—have insights based on traditions passed down the generations. However, when evaluating present-day interpretations, one must take into account that thirty to forty generations have passed since the petroglyphs were made.

Still, some studies produce valuable insights. Patination and style analyses conclude that all the V-Bar-V petroglyphs are Sinagua and are roughly contemporaneous, having been made sometime between A.D. 1150 and 1400. This contrasts to sites like Newspaper Rock (p. 176), whose glyphs were made by numerous cultural groups over thousands of years. The contemporaneity of the images is indicated by their similar style, equal degree of patination (weathering), and lack of superimposition.

The V-Bar-V petroglyphs include anthropomorphic figures; animals, snakes, and birds; and geometric forms. An unusual aspect of this panel is how close the pictures are to each other, frequently touching or connected by wandering lines. This interconnectivity suggests that the individual elements may contribute to an intended meaning of the whole, as if stories were being told.

Another interesting characteristic is the presence of many small cupules (cup-like indentations) pecked into the bodies of other elements, especially human-like and animal figures, often in vital areas such as the chest. Do the cupules reflect attempts to obtain power from the figures?

*Detail of the main petroglyph panel at the V-Bar-V Ranch site.*

From the V-Bar-V site's parking lot, a short, flat, well-marked trail leads to the petroglyph panels. A ranger or docent on duty will answer your questions. Although the petroglyphs are accessible to photograph, they are shaded by the cliff and trees. You will need about an hour here. Be sure to visit Montezuma Well (p. 161), only about six miles away, and Montezuma Castle (p. 159), also nearby. Travel services are available in Sedona and Camp Verde.

Suggested reading: *People of the Verde Valley*, edited by Stephen Trimble, Museum of Northern Arizona, Flagstaff, Arizona, 1981.

# Montezuma Castle National Monument

*Montezuma Castle National Monument is just north of Camp Verde, Arizona, 50 miles south of Flagstaff. From Interstate 17, take Exit 289. Information: (520) 567-3322. Entrance fee.*

Contrary to past popular belief, Montezuma, the sixteenth-century Aztec ruler, was never exiled to northern Arizona. Had such a fate befallen him, however, no more fitting domicile could he have wished for than the "castle" that today bears his name. Impregnably situated on the ledges of a sheer cliff overlooking Beaver Creek in the lush Verde Valley, this cliff dwelling is a striking example of precolumbian American architecture. Its seventeen rooms, which are in excellent condition, reach up to five stories, presenting a dramatic view from below.

Sinagua culture appeared in the Verde Valley around A.D. 700. Montezuma Castle, however, did not come under construction until the early 1100s and was not completed for at least another century. By this time, the region had become quite heavily populated. People here grew corn, squash, beans, and cotton in fields that they irrigated from Beaver Creek. You will see this stream from the trail. Like the inhabitants of Tuzigoot (p. 163) and other pueblos in the region, those of Montezuma Castle participated in widespread trade—both foreign and domestic, as it were. Some of the crafts they produced are exhibited in the visitor center.

The castle, protected by a deep overhang in the cliff's face, is built of small limestone blocks laid in mortar and roofed by sycamore timbers overlaid by poles, sticks, grass, and several inches of mud. Today, we can only imagine the effort required to haul these heavy materials up the cliff. The outside rooms sit nearly flush with the high ledges and form a concave arc that conforms to the surrounding cave.

Two paths, one from the valley floor, which required the use of ladders, and one from the side of the cliff, joined to enter the cliff dwelling. At the junction sits a small smoke-blackened room believed to have been a sentry post. Compact inner rooms with small doorways conserved heat and made hostile entry all but impossible. Two other factors enhanced heating: The site faces south and sits far above the colder air that settles on the valley floor below. While excavated remains of corn, beans, squash, and cotton are evidence of agricultural activity, other plant remains, such as seeds, nuts, and agave, indicate that the Sinagua who lived here continued to forage for food.

The castle had a relatively brief occupancy. Scholars do not yet understand why the Sinagua left the Verde Valley. In drought conditions, this would have been a natural gathering place. Perhaps overcrowding caused internal dissentions to develop, or worse, disease. Unsanitary conditions around a densely occupied pueblo can create the conditions

for infectious diseases. Foreign invasion is a possibility, but no evidence of warfare exists, and the Yavapai and Apaches did not arrive until sometime later. The unknowns of the past draw many students to the field of archaeology: Maybe one of these students will solve the riddle of why the Sinagua left their Verde Valley homes.

In the 1880s, before archaeology had become a science, Montezuma Castle was stripped of its well-preserved contents by a collector from nearby Forte Verde. Castle A, which is located one hundred yards away at the base of the cliff, however, was more systematically excavated in the 1930s. This once five-story pueblo (twice the size of Montezuma Castle) collapsed in a conflagration while still being inhabited. Excavators found many burials here, one of which held a stunning array of jewelry. The dead person, a woman in her thirties, must have been held in special regard by her contemporaries.

Because of its fragility, the castle may no longer be entered. A paved pathway about a quarter of a mile in length takes you from the visitor center to an excellent viewpoint, continues to Castle A, and loops back along Beaver Creek. It is an easy, pleasant walk. It will take you about half an hour, perhaps longer if you stop to take pictures or relax in the shade of the sycamore trees. And do not expect to be alone; the monument accommodates hundreds of tourists each day.

## Montezuma Well

Sunk into a hill six miles north of Montezuma Castle is one of the most unusual geologic spots in the Southwest. Known as Montezuma Well, it is a limestone sink, 470 feet in diameter. Ducks swim on the serene surface of this small, round lake and coots poke along its reedy shores. Through its outlet flow a million and a half gallons of water per day. Little wonder that this was a popular place for the Hohokam and Sinagua to live.

The area around the well was first permanently settled by Hohokam people in the seventh century and remained inhabited, later by the Sinagua, through the 1400s. They took advantage of the strong flow of water from the sinkhole to dig a network of irrigation ditches leading to their fields. The population around Montezuma Well probably peaked around A.D. 1300 when, it seems, everyone drew together for security: another hint that some external foe may have threatened their way of life.

A short trail leads to the rim of the hill, where you will have a view of the lake and some cliff dwellings. You can walk down to the water's edge, passing some habitations in caves, or along the rim to find more ruins, or down the back side to see where the overflow water gushes out from the lake to form a creek. At 76 degrees, the water has created its own lush mini-environment.

*Montezuma Castle.*

*Montezuma Well.*

Along the road to Montezuma Well, you will pass the roofed-over remains of a Hohokam pithouse, one of the few in the Southwest that has been preserved intact. Its walls and roof, of course, decomposed long ago, but you can see the floor features and a scale model of how it looked when in use.

Restaurant and travel accommodations are available at Camp Verde and near most other interstate exits. An interesting counterpart to this monument is Tuzigoot, located near Clarkdale. In addition, the V-Bar-V Ranch Petroglyph Site (p. 157) is only a few miles away.

Suggested reading: *Ruins along the River,* by Carle Hodge, Southwest Parks and Monuments Association, Tucson, Arizona, 1986.

# Tuzigoot National Monument

*Tuzigoot National Monument is along U.S. 89A between Cottonwood and Clarkdale, Arizona. Information: (520) 634-5564. Entrance fee.*

The marked dissimilarity of Arizona's Sinagua monuments—Wupatki, Elden, Walnut Canyon, Montezuma Castle, Tuzigoot—speak to the very nature of Sinagua culture. The Sinagua were, indeed, people in between, influenced in many ways by their neighbors.

Tuzigoot is a hill town. The remains of its buildings cover a 120-foot-high limestone ridge overlooking the meandering Verde River. This river, which begins in high country twenty-five miles to the north, flows into the Salt River near Phoenix. The first European to describe the Rio Verde was the Spaniard Antonio de Espejo, whose explorations led him on a wide-ranging journey through the Southwest. His Hopi guides led him along the Palatkwapi Trail to the Verde Valley and showed him nearby quarries, which Native Americans had long exploited. Centuries later, one of these would become the site of the famous mining town of Jerome. When you visit the national monument, you will notice the effects of recent large-scale mining just below Tuzigoot hill.

From its beginnings around A.D. 1000 as a small cluster of houses, Tuzigoot experienced growth spurts in the 1200s and 1300s. By this time, the building complex had about ninety rooms housing some two hundred people. Several other similarly fortified communities were visible from the pueblo's elevation and many more dotted the landscape.

The Verde Valley had numerous advantages for living then, as it does today. Its climate was ideal: It was well watered by the Verde and its tributaries; its soils were excellent for farming; and it had a long growing season. Given such conditions, one wonders why the Sinagua started farming so late, after A.D. 700. Within a century, Hohokam people moved up to this valley from their Salt River communities around present-

*Tuzigoot ruins above the Verde Valley.*

day Phoenix. Archaeologists believe it was they who taught the Sinagua how to use irrigation, a farming method they had already been practicing successfully for a long time.

The people of Tuzigoot grew cotton and a variety of food products in the valley and extracted minerals such as argillite, salt, and copper from mines they controlled. With such resources, they were able to establish a lucrative regional and foreign trade, importing turquoise and finely decorated pottery from nearby, parrot feathers from Mexico, shells from the Pacific Coast, and fine jewelry, which itself was tradable.

The Verde Valley people, including the inhabitants of Tuzigoot, left around A.D. 1400. It is believed they migrated north and east to

Anderson Mesa, Chavez Pass, and the Hopi Mesas. Some Verde Valley descendants probably inhabited the Homol'ovi villages (p. 106) near Winslow, Arizona.

The archaeological excavations at Tuzigoot were a Depression-era project. Between 1933 and 1934, Louis Caywood and Edward Spicer, graduate students from the University of Arizona, hired as many as forty-eight laborers to dig out all the rooms in the pueblo. Then, using a school building in nearby Clarkdale, the artifacts were cleaned and catalogued prior to be shipped to a museum. As a result of this methodology, many potentially valuable scientific data about Tuzigoot's cultural history were left unrecorded and no parts of the site remained undisturbed for future study.

You will appreciate Tuzigoot National Monument's visitor center and museum. The building itself dates from the 1930s, and its interesting exhibits are shown in hand-crafted wood-and-glass display cabinets. There is also an informative Tuzigoot room reconstruction to see. You should plan an hour or so to see the museum and tour the site. The ruins trail is only a quarter of a mile long.

Picnic tables are set up outside the visitor center. Camping is available at nearby Dead Horse Ranch State Park, and you will find many travel services within a few miles. Montezuma Castle National Monument (p. 159) is only a short distance away, and the town of Jerome makes an interesting and scenic excursion.

Suggested reading: *Tuzigoot National Monument,* by Rose Houk, Southwest Parks and Monuments Association, Tucson, Arizona, 1995.

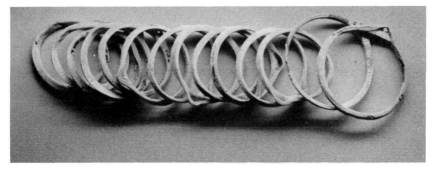

*Shell bracelets, Tuzigoot Museum.*

# Tonto National Monument

*Tonto National Monument is located on Arizona 88, 2 miles east of Roosevelt and 30 miles northwest of Globe, Arizona. Driving time from Phoenix is about 2 hours. Information: (520) 467-2241. Entrance Fee.*

The Salado residents of the cliff dwellings in Tonto National Monument had a spectacular view over the broad Tonto Basin through which the Salt River once meandered. In 1911, the Salt was dammed to create Roosevelt Reservoir. While this landscape has been greatly altered since the old days, the view from the ruins still is breathtaking.

Twelve hundred years ago, it is believed, Hohokam settlers from far downstream moved up to the Tonto Basin, where they built small pit-house villages, grew crops in the river's floodplain, and stayed about three hundred years. Beginning in the mid-1100s, archaeologists have noted, some changes occurred in the style of local pottery and architecture. Whether these modifications represent an evolution of local Hohokam culture or an influx of new people is a matter not yet resolved, but they are called Salado after the nearby Rio Salado or Salt River.

At an elevation of just over three thousand feet (the lower cliff house) and still lower in the Basin, the Hohokam and Salado enjoyed a most comfortable climate. They also benefitted from a three-hundred-day growing season during which they raised corn, pumpkins, squash, gourds, several varieties of beans, cotton, and grain amaranth. In addition, between the basin and the hills, they harvested a wide variety of native plants, including cactus fruit, piñon nuts and acorns, mesquite beans, wild grapes, and various seeds. Still other plants provided medicinal herbs, fiber for clothing, and wood for building houses. No wonder that skeletal remains recovered here show the Salado of the Tonto Basin to have been a strong, healthy people.

In the mid-1200s, many people from the basin relocated to higher elevations where they built fortified cliff dwellings. One wonders what pressures moved them to live so far from their croplands. However, the dry caves that provided them shelter in the uplands were a perfect environment to preserve nearly everything they eventually left behind. Archaeologists (and unfortunately looters before them) have rarely found the remains of perishable organic artifacts in such good condition. Ethnobotanist Vorsila Bohrer commented, "the plant material [at Tonto]...is perfectly preserved. Dried lima beans look like ones that might have come in a cellophane package on the grocery shelf."

The cave sites also contained some of the finest examples of textiles woven of cotton, yucca, and hair ever recovered in the Southwest. The

*Lower Ruins, Tonto National Monument.*

monument's three major sites—Lower Ruin, Lower Ruin Annex, and Upper Ruin—also yielded plaited yucca-leaf sandals, basketry, matting, and cordage. Researchers found a thirty-inch bow of netleaf hackberry (a tough, bending wood), arrows, clubs, and such household items as fire-making equipment, fiber pot rests, brushes, torches, stirring sticks, tattoo needles, gums and adhesives, and spinning and weaving implements. Ceremonial items found included prayer sticks, charms, paint daubers, reed cigarettes, dice, and a bow.

From the visitor center, a one-mile round-trip trail leads to Lower Ruin. You will need an hour or longer for this walk and to see the cliff dwelling. To join a ranger-led tour to Upper Ruin, you should make reservations in advance. That excursion takes about three hours.

Food and lodging are available in Roosevelt and there are camping places nearby. An additional attraction is the scenic drive on Arizona 88 from Apache Junction to Roosevelt. This tortuous road, which is unpaved in some sections, offers stunning desert and mountain views. Be warned, however, that some sections are closed to vehicles over thirty feet in length and driving is slow. Other ruins in the vicinity are Casa Grande (p. 41) and Besh Ba Gowah (below).

Suggested reading: *Archaeological Studies at Tonto National Monument, Arizona*, by Charlie R. Steen et al., Southwestern Monuments Association, Gila Pueblo, Globe, Arizona, 1962.

# Besh Ba Gowah Archaeological Park

*Besh Ba Gowah Archaeological Park is in Globe, Arizona, 87 miles east of Phoenix. From U.S. 60, take the Broad Street exit and turn right on Jess Hayes Road. Follow signs to the park. Information: (520) 425-0320. Fee.*

*Besh Ba Gowah* is an Apache word meaning "place of metal," referring to the intensive copper mining operations in the Globe area in historic times. The archaeological site, however, consists of the remains of a Salado village, which included about 250 ground floor rooms and several plazas. The entire village may have contained as many as 450 rooms when it was occupied between A.D. 1225 and 1450. Thus, it represents a major regional archaeological resource.

The village sits on a ridge overlooking Pinal Creek, a tributary of the Salt River, and is surrounded by the eight-thousand-foot Pinal Mountains to the southwest and the Apache Mountains to the north. The presence of numerous other ruins in the vicinity suggests a large local population.

Besh Ba Gowah's buildings were constructed of unshaped granite cobbles set in thick clay mortar. Excavations have uncovered many small rooms believed to have been used for storage, larger residential

*Besh Ba Gowah Ruins.*

rooms averaging 225 square feet, and some even more spacious rooms of unknown function. The presence at the site of stored beans and corn, as well as many stone hoes, indicates that its inhabitants farmed, probably in fields along Pinal Creek. They were also fine crafts people and traded actively with other villages in the area, as well as with people who lived as far away as Mexico and the Pacific Coast.

Salado culture is considered to be a blend of native or local traditions with influences from the Hohokam and Pueblo cultures. The presence at Besh Ba Gowah of a Hohokam component underneath the Salado ruins is proof that Hohokam people were here first, or that Hohokam culture evolved into what archaeologists refer to as Salado.

Besh Ba Gowah originally was surveyed and recorded in 1883 by the archaeological explorer, Adolph F. Bandelier, while he was waiting in Globe for Apache hostilities to subside. He described the site's Salado character through its ceramics. Irene S. Vickery conducted the first formal archaeological investigations at the site beginning in 1935 as a Federal Emergency Relief Administration project. Vickery uncovered more than one hundred rooms and recovered 350 Salado burials. Sadly, she died before publishing the results of her work, and for many years, the ruins lay unattended and little appreciated.

In 1948, the Boy Scouts of America selected Besh Ba Gowah ruins to be the site of their national jamboree, and in order to accommodate their camping needs, the Army Corps of Engineers bulldozed and leveled the northern portion of the ruins. The City of Globe subsequently developed this area into a city park and later bulldozed more of the ruins to make room for recreational facilities.

In 1984, with the area's mining economy in decline, the city began redeveloping the site and park complex to attract tourists. To carry out this plan, it engaged the services of professional archaeologists. Under the direction of John H. Hohmann, the site was mapped, excavated, stabilized, and partially reconstructed. Other additions were a museum and an interpretive trail through the ruins.

As you walk through the ruins, you will pass through reconstructed corridors and climb a ladder to second-story rooms. The experience offers a sense of what this pueblo was originally like. One notable feature along the way is a large square subterranean room, with benches along the wall, that apparently was used for religious ceremonies. It had an altar and a sipapu (a symbolic entrance hole leading to the underworld), which was found filled with ground turquoise and sealed with a large quartz crystal. Besh Ba Gowah's museum contains a reconstructed model of the pueblo, numerous examples of Gila Polychrome and other types of regionally made pottery, and prehistoric implements.

The transformation of Besh Ba Gowah from overgrown and looted mounds to an interpreted archaeological park reflects the growing public interest and pride in America's rich aboriginal heritage. Today, this site, which is managed by the City of Globe, is a rewarding place to visit, where you can learn much about the little-known Salado culture.

Travel services are available in Globe. While here, you may also wish to make a side trip to Tonto National Monument (p. 167).

Suggested reading: "Besh Ba Gowah," by Irene Vickery, *The Kiva*, vol. 4, no. 5, 1939.

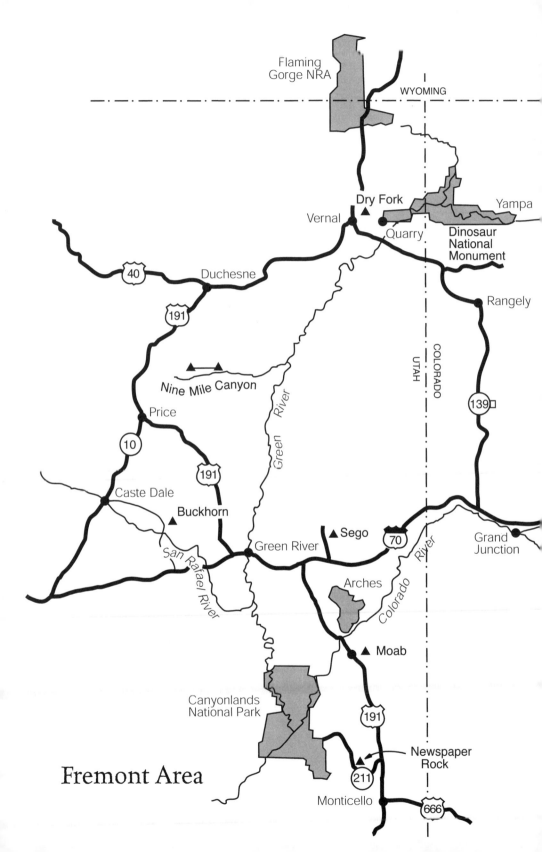

Flaming
Gorge NRA

WYOMING

Dry Fork ▲

Vernal

Quarry

Yampa

Dinosaur
National
Monument

Duchesne

40

191

Rangely

Nine Mile Canyon ▲——▲

Green River

UTAH | COLORADO

Price

10

191

139 ▫

Caste Dale

Buckhorn ▲

San Rafael River

▲ Sego

Green River

70

Colorado River

Grand
Junction

Arches

Canyonlands
National Park

▲ Moab

191

Newspaper
Rock

▲

211

666

Monticello

# Fremont Area

# The Fremont
## Rock Artists of the North

Among the Southwest's prehistoric peoples, the Fremont should receive a special award for having best succeeded in confounding archaeologists. Ever since the Fremont culture was first defined in 1931 by a Harvard graduate student named Noel Morss, scholars have argued about its origins, characteristics, fate, and even its existence as a distinct culture. Since these people (named after an American explorer and nearby river) knew exactly who they were and what they were doing, they would certainly get a chuckle at the confusion they managed to create in a later Euro-scientific culture.

The principal archaeological trait of the Fremont culture—all scholars agree on this—is a thin-walled, plain gray pottery, variations of which have been found at sites throughout most of Utah, the eastern part of Nevada, and the western edge of Colorado. On a topographical map, the eastern Great Basin and western Colorado Plateau would roughly delineate the Fremont culture area.

The Fremont produced a few other distinctive artifacts besides plain gray pots: One was a particular style of baskets, another a unique type of moccasin. The most compelling trait, however, was an artistic style that is exemplified in both clay figurines and rock art. It is the latter that remains so dramatically visible in the land where they lived. What intrigues viewers the most are the bold anthropomorphic figures with their broad shoulders and trapezoidal bodies, who sport elaborate headdresses, fine jewelry, and fashionable clothing.

The field of archaeology traditionally has described ancient cultures by the style of objects found in sites. From these surviving "things," scholars form theories about how a given culture developed and even how its

members behaved. With so few distinctively Fremont artifacts, archaeologists have difficulty defining who the Fremont people really were.

Some scholars have viewed the Fremont as a backward fringe group of Anasazi who migrated or were pushed northward beyond the Anasazi heartland. Others have proposed that they were Athapaskan (ancestral Apache/Navajo) bison hunters who migrated south into what is now Utah around A.D. 500. A third theory, which is shared by most researchers, holds that the Fremont emerged from an existing regional nomadic hunter-gatherer population. This emergence, signified by the adoption of agriculture and building of permanent houses, happened as early as A.D. 400 in some localities and as late as 900 in others.

*Similarities of form are evident in the Fremont clay figure from San Rafael Swell (right) and the petroglyph in Dry Fork Canyon (above). Figurine photo courtesy Peabody Museum, Harvard University.*

The Fremont, apparently, were very flexible and adaptive in their way of life. They farmed when conditions were favorable for agriculture but were always ready to return to hunting and foraging when crops failed. Fremont farmers built settlements where they irrigated fields, made pottery, used grinding stones, and erected crude structures of mud, stone, and wood. When conditions drew them to a more mobile life style, they built temporary structures or found shelter in caves and rock alcoves. Through the seasons and over the centuries, the Fremont exploited a wide variety of environments; their sites are found from the game-rich uplands of the western slopes of the Rockies to the marshy shores of shallow lakes in the Great Basin. Their ability to survive lay in their willingness to adapt.

What happened to the Fremont is as debatable as where they came from. Their culture began to disappear around A.D. 1250 and no archaeological trace of it can be found dating past 1450. Possibly they gave up agriculture and went back to their roaming life as hunter-gatherers. They also may have been absorbed by new peoples, such as the Numic-speaking Utes, Paiutes, and Shoshonis, who migrated into what is now Utah sometime after A.D. 1000.

While Fremont village sites are of much interest to archaeologists, they are not the stuff of public monuments. Not built to endure, they tended to melt back into the ground. Some of the petroglyph and pictograph panels that they created, on the other hand, have survived and form a fascinating collection of ancient American art. When you see the tall, broad-shouldered, anthropomorphic figures that the Fremont left on cliff walls, you will be impressed. These expressions of an ancient culture cut through archaeological confusions. They speak directly to you, one people to another.

Suggested reading: *Exploring the Fremont*, by David B. Madsen, Utah Museum of Natural History, Salt Lake City, Utah, 1989.

# Newspaper Rock

*Newspaper Rock is an historical monument in southeastern Utah, located along the north side of Utah 211, 12 miles west of its intersection with U.S. 163, north of Monticello. Information: (435) 587-1532.*

No rock art panel could be more jam-packed with petroglyphs than Newspaper Rock, which is on the way to the Needles District of Canyonlands National Park. On this darkly patinated slab of sandstone are hundreds of figures and designs from several Native American cultures—Archaic, Basketmaker, Fremont, Anasazi, Ute, and Navajo—as well as some Spanish and Anglo American contributions. The glyphs are protected from the elements by a natural overhang that seems to have been custom-made for the purpose.

*Newspaper Rock.*

The author includes this site in the Fremont section of the present book because it was on the Anasazi-Fremont frontier and, as you drive north from the Four Corners region, it is the first place to find strong examples of Fremont rock art.

Rock art researchers have long been perplexed by how to accurately date petroglyphs. Sometimes they can date a particular rock art site by its association with a nearby ruin for which definite dates are known. Since there are no ruins here, this method is of little use at Newspaper Rock, but another is. You will note the presence of horses and riders on the panel. Native American horses became extinct thousands of years ago but horses were reintroduced to the Americas by Europeans in historic times. Ute Indians brought them to this part of Utah sometime after the 1680 Pueblo Revolt in New Mexico.

Knowing which rock art styles are associated with which cultures also helps in dating. Newspaper Rock contains some pictures that are in a style known to be from the Archaic period, which ended two thousand years ago. The style of other images clearly identifies them with the Fremont Indians, who lived here between around A.D. 500 and 1300. Through style comparisons and other methods, scholars are building up a body of knowledge about the dates of widely scattered rock art sites.

Regardless of academic insights, petroglyphs and pictographs can be appreciated on their own merits by just about anyone. Some images seem clear in meaning, some obscure; some are carefully executed, others sloppily scrawled; some seem to tell a story, others are abstract patterns. You will see examples of many styles and viewpoints at Newspaper Rock. While this site may not have been a newspaper, it still contains much to read: You can glance at the panel for five minutes or study it for an hour.

Another panel of petroglyphs can be found in nearby Shay Canyon. This one contains anthropomorphic figures, bighorn sheep, birds, and abstract designs. To reach it, continue west on Route 211 to an informal pullout exactly two miles from Newspaper Rock. From there a rough trail leads down an embankment, crosses a streambed and flat area, and climbs up a short talus slope to some cliffs where the glyphs are clearly visible. The walk is about three hundred yards from the road. Do not touch the petroglyphs as the oils and acids in your hands can further their deterioration and contaminate them for dating research.

Suggested reading: *Indian Rock Art of the Southwest,* by Polly Schaafsma, University of New Mexico Press, Albuquerque, New Mexico, 1980.

## Moab Area Rock Art Sites

*Moab is a resort town along U.S. 191 in southeastern Utah. Several rock art sites, which are described individually, are easily accessible from downtown. Information: (800) 635-6622.*

Numerous rock art panels can be found in the vicinity of Moab. This chapter introduces you to three sites, which are easily accessible from town. However, if you are hiking, bicycling, river-running, or just on a driving tour, keep your eyes open and you will probably discover more.

Little is known about the Fremont culture due to the fact that it has not been studied in nearly the depth or detail as that of the Anasazi. Unlike Anasazi ruins, Fremont sites are difficult to date with precision. This is due in part to the scarcity of dateable wood recovered from them.

The Southern San Raphael branch of the Fremont Indians lived on the northern periphery of the Colorado Plateau, north of the Anasazi, between around A.D. 500 and 1300. In its final centuries the Fremont culture overlapped that of the Anasazi when the latter was at its height. At the rock art sites around Moab, you can recognize the influence of the Fremonts' neighbors to the south. Some of the glyphs, indeed, may have been made by the Anasazi themselves. Often you can also see a resemblance between the anthropomorphic figures of the Fremont and those of their Archaic predecessors who made the large Barrier Canyon

*Petroglyphs along Potash Road.*

Style figures in Canyonlands (p. 76), Buckhorn Wash (p. 11), and sites in Capitol Reef National Monument.

## Potash Road Petroglyphs

*The Potash Road Petroglyphs are located along the north side of Utah 279, 9 miles west of Moab. Follow Utah 191 for 4 miles north of town, turn west on 279, and continue 5.5 miles where road signs mark three petroglyph areas.*

On the Potash Road petroglyph panels, you will see rows of triangle-shaped human figures holding hands and possibly dancing. Some wear horned headresses or carry spears and shields. Also present are animal forms, including bighorn sheep, deer and a huge bear, and various non-representational designs. In addition, you can find horsemen: These figures were probably made by Ute Indians, who lived in this region after the Fremont had gone.

Potash Road follows the north side of the Colorado River. Across the river, you will enjoy a view of dramatic sandstone cliffs topped by bluffs of fossil sand dunes. The Colorado flows south from here to its confluence with the Green. Together they pick up speed through Cataract Canyon, then empty into Lake Powell.

## Courthouse Wash Rock Art

*To find the Courthouse Wash rock art, drive 4 miles north of Moab on U.S. 191, crossing the Colorado River and Courthouse Wash, to a parking lot on the right side of the highway. From here, a well-marked foot path leads a half a mile back across the wash to the site.*

This rock art site, which includes several striking pictographs and some petroglyphs, is located along the base of a cliff and on rock slabs just above the confluence of Courthouse Wash and the Colorado River. Though the site was heavily vandalized in the past, recent conservation work has much improved its appearance.

You will immediately be struck by two large, stylized pictographs of anthropomorphs, who appear to be holding two large white circles with vertical blue lines through them. The head of one figure resembles an upended horseshoe, the other has pointed horns or ears. While these figures bear some likeness to Fremont anthropomorphs, they more closely reflect the Barrier Canyon Style, which is from an earlier period. This site also has petroglyphs of a variety of animal, bird, and abstract elements. As they reflect Fremont and Anasazi styles, it is thought this locality was active as a rock art site for a long time.

## Golf Course Petroglyphs

*This petroglyph panel is located near the northeast corner of the Moab Golf Course. From the corner of Main and Center streets, take U.S. 191 south 4 miles to the golf course turnoff. Turn left on Spanish Trail Road, proceed approximately 1 mile and turn right on Westwater Drive, then continue .5 miles to a small pullout on the left side of the road.*

The Golf Course Petroglyphs site is an extensive Fremont panel (with Anasazi influence) on the face of a large sandstone rock. Starting at ground level (possibly below ground level), the glyphs, including anthropomorphic figures, reach up about thirty feet on the wall. Some wear horn, antler, and feathered headdresses and have dangling ear-bobs. Bighorn sheep, deer, elk, and various wavy lines also can be seen. The site is unmolested by vandals; however, natural erosion has obliterated some drawings.

Other rock art sites near Moab you may wish to visit are at Sego

*Dinosaur bones at the quarry.*

Canyon (p. 13) and Newspaper Rock (p. 176). In Moab you will find a wide choice of restaurants and accomodations and many travel services and tour companies.

> Suggested reading: *Petroglyphs and Pictographs of Utah,* Volume One, by Kenneth B. Castleton, Utah Museum of Natural History, Salt Lake City, 1984.

# Dinosaur National Monument

*Dinosaur National Monument straddles the border of northeastern Utah and northwestern Colorado. From Vernal, Utah, take U.S. 40 east for 12 miles to Jensen, then drive 7 miles north on Utah 149 to the monument entrance that leads to the dinosaur quarry. Information: (970) 374-3000. Entrance fee, April to October.*

Dinosaur National Monument, located east of Vernal, Utah, is world-renowned for its quarry of fossil dinosaur bones. Paleontologists stopped excavating this site some years ago; however, they left a portion of the quarry in place with hundreds of dinosaur bones still visible in the cliff face. The National Park Service built a museum around the quarry, which also features exhibits and dinosaur skeletons and models. This unique museum offers a fascinating window into the time when these awesome creatures roamed the western United States 150 million years ago.

Less known within this park, but nonetheless of much interest, are numerous archaeological sites relating to the region's human past. Some of these sites are open to visitation and are accessible by driving and hiking or by river rafting. The Dinosaur region has been inhabited by people for thousands of years. Hunter-gathers roamed the mesas, canyons, and river drainages more than a millenium ago, finding shelter in caves and rock shelters. By A.D. 650, Fremont people were practicing horticulture while continuing to hunt and forage in the manner of their semi-nomadic predecessors. Still later, Ute Indians revisited some of the same alcoves that had been used by earlier people.

## Swelter Shelter and Cub Creek Petroglyphs

*Swelter Shelter, located along the road a mile east of the dinosaur quarry turnoff, is a very accessible site. From the parking area, you follow a short, level path to a shallow alcove, which provided shelter to Archaic and Fremont people from around 7000 B.C. to A.D. 1250.*

Archaeologists who excavated the shelter's floor between 1964 and 1965, encountered numerous difficulties. For one, its south-facing exposure causes it to heat up considerably. While this may have been advantageous to its ancient occupants in winter, members of the archaeological crew, who worked here in the summer months, found themselves sweltering and thus gave the site its name.

The lack of stratigraphy in the shelter's floor complicated the archaeologists' job of cultural interpretation. They excavated two hearths and a collection of flaked stone tools, including projectile points, knife blades, drills, scrapers, and hammer stones. These artifacts provided the means to roughly date the shelter's long period of use.

While Fremont people did not live in Swelter Shelter, they probably used it as a campsite. When here, they pecked images on its walls—many now are faint—including human figures, deer and other animals, and random patterns. The park service has installed interpretive signs along the trail. Plan twenty minutes or so to visit this site.

The Cub Creek Petroglyphs also are along the left side of Cub Creek Road, 9.6 miles beyond Swelter Shelter and one mile before you come

*McKee Spring petroglyphs.*

to the Josie Morris Cabin. These glyphs represent the Classic Vernal Style of Fremont rock art and are thought to date to around A.D. 1000. Like Swelter Shelter, they include anthropomorphic figures, animals, and other designs. From this site, walk a hundred yards or so further up the road and you will be able to spot two large petroglyphs of lizards on a rock high up the slope to the left. Binoculars will help. The size and subject matter of these glyphs are highly unusual.

## McKee Spring Petroglyphs

*The petroglyphs at McKee Spring can be found along the Island Park Road. From Jensen, drive north on Utah 149 and turn left on Brush Creek Road. At 4.8 miles, turn right on Island Park Road, which is unpaved and impassible in wet weather. After 4 miles, bear right and continue 11 miles to where the road narrows. Here you will see a petroglyph panel on the right with anthropomorphic figures, two buffalo, and other markings.*

About a quarter of a mile beyond this panel, walk up to the edge of the mesa on the left (north side), where you will find several outstanding petroglyph panels, including an anthropomorhic figure bearing a

*Pictographs at Deluge Shelter.*

shield, which has been widely reproduced in rock art books. The McKee Spring and Dry Fork Canyon (p. 186) localities are the two type sites for the Classic Vernal Style of Fremont rock art. If you continue another mile beyond McKee Spring, you will reach a spot along the Green River where many rafters and kayakers launch to run the rapids through Split Mountain.

## Deluge Shelter Pictographs

*The Deluge Shelter pictographs are along the Jones Hole Trail, which follows Jones Hole Creek from the Jones Hole Fish Hatchery to the Green River. From just east of Vernal, take the Diamond Mountain Road forty miles to the hatchery and trailhead. The pictographs are a mile and three quarters down the trail on the right. The trail is well marked and interpretive signs have been placed at the site.*

Archaeologists excavated Deluge Shelter in 1966 and 1967, finding fifteen levels of cultural material buried in ten feet of floor deposits.

They named it after Jones Creek flooded and inundated the site. The lowest level showed a 5000–4000 B.C. occupation. The Fremont, who painted the pictures on the cliff, used it in the tenth century A.D., and other Indians, probably Utes, came here after A.D. 1300. Shallow alcoves like this one offered enough protection to serve as a dry camp for transient hunters. Excavated artifacts included stone beads and pipes; bone awls, pendants, and gaming pieces; antler flakers; and pottery.

The pictographs, painted in reddish-brown pigments, show human and animal figures and abstract patterns, one of which resembles a long fishing or hunting net. Whether or not it was really meant to depict a net is impossible to know; it is interesting to note, however, that unlike the Anasazi–Pueblo Indians, the Utes and Paiutes, who inhabited the eastern Great Basin in historic times, were expert fishermen.

Like all rock art, these pictographs are extremely fragile and must not be touched. The Park Service maintains a campground about a mile below the pictograph site. Reservations and a backcountry permit are required and can be obtained at the Dinosaur Quarry. You can also hike up to Deluge Shelter from the confluence of Jones Hole Creek and the Green River. Be sure to bring adequate water, food, and clothing.

## Archaeological Sites along the Yampa River

Another way to experience archaeological sites in Dinosaur National Monument is by taking a rafting trip down the Yampa and Green rivers. (The Yampa is the last free-flowing tributary of the Colorado River.) Commercial companies in Vernal run river trips in the spring, or you can apply to the National Park Service for a private permit. Rafters begin their trip at Deerlodge Park on the Yampa, float down to Echo Park and the confluence with the Green River, then continue through Whirlpool Canyon and Split Mountain to the exit near the Dinosaur Quarry. Commercial companies offer trips lasting three, four, or five days.

It helps to have someone in your group who knows the history and archaeology along these rivers. Most commercial river guides, however, are familiar with Mantle Cave, located up a short draw off the Yampa in the area known as Castle Park. Mantle Cave is a huge, vaulted, north-facing alcove that was systematically excavated (after being repeatedly looted) in 1940. It contained four dozen storage chambers, ranging from lined and lidded bell-shaped cysts, to masonry granaries, to large slab-lined pits. They held a wealth of material, some of which was ceremonial in nature. In one cache, researchers found a deer-scalp headdress with attached ears that had quill ribs to make them stand rigid. Another held an ermine pelt in winter pelage. The most remarkable find, however, was a ceremonial headdress made of 370 flicker feathers and a white ermine headband that resembles headdresses depicted in Fremont rock art. It was radiocarbon dated to A.D. 1250.

Petroglyphs can be found in Echo Park at the confluence of the Yampa and Green rivers. Some are visible from the river on the east face of Steamboat Rock and around the corner. From the Echo Park ranger station, walk a few hundred yards up the road and you will find a short trail on the right, which leads to a panel of petroglyphs. Curiously, they seem more Anasazi in style than Fremont. Continue a little further up the road and you will come to Whispering Cave, a pleasantly cool place to escape the sun's heat. Look for bighorn sheep along the way.

Dinosaur National Monument is justifiably famed for its spectacular scenery and fascinating dinosaur museum. However, if you plan to spend time here on a car tour, hiking backcountry trails, or river rafting, your experience will be much enhanced if you learn about the region's human history.

Vernal, Utah, offers a wide selection of motels and restaurants as well as tour and river-rafting companies. While here, a trip to the Dry Fork Canyon Indian Petroglyphs (below) is recommended, as is a visit to the Utah State Natural History Museum on Main Street.

Suggested reading: "Fremont Cultures," by John P. Marwitt in *Handbook of North American Indians,* Volume 11, edited by Warren L. D'Azevedo, Smithsonian Institution, Washington, D.C., 1986.

# Dry Fork Canyon Petroglyphs

*The Dry Fork Canyon petroglyphs are located on the McConkie Ranch, 10 miles northeast of Vernal, Utah. From Main Street, go north on 500 West to Utah 121. Turn right (north) on 3500 West (Dry Fork Canyon) and continue to the Indian Petroglyphs turnoff (McConkie Ranch) on the right. A parking area is provided. Information: (800) 837-6258. Entrance fee.*

The most outstanding accessible collection of Fremont rock art is on the private McConkie Ranch just outside Vernal. This is the type site for the Classic Vernal Style, which represents the apex of Fremont petroglyphic art. We are indebted to the McConkie Ranch owner for allowing the public to see these petroglyphs.

When you park here, stop at the tiny visitors' hut for information and to pay a nominal fee for trail upkeep. The trail begins behind the building. It is a minimally improved path, which goes to a series of glyphs up the slope to the right, then loops back to the left and leads to several panels of large, imposing anthropomorphic figures. Plan about one and a half hours for this walk. A second petroglyph walking tour starts across the ranch road, traverses a meadow, and goes by numerous pictures pecked

*Anthropomorphic figure, Dry Fork Canyon.*

along the cliff base among the piñon and juniper trees. It then crosses a field of sage and ends with a view of the famous Three Kings site high on a cliff. Binoculars greatly help to see this spectacular panel in its full detail. The second hike also takes about an hour and a half.

The most impressive petroglyphs you will see on these walks are representations of tall, broad-shouldered, human-like figures. Typically, they have large rectangular or bucket-like heads on tapered torsos. Their slit or dot eyes, some with tear streaks, look straight at you. Many wear elaborate headgear and earrings or earbobs. Around their necks hang necklaces of beads or what appear to be heavy shell pendants. The ornamental detail in their stylized costumes, executed with stone tools, shows the finest petroglyphic technique. In her book, *The Rock Art of Utah*, Polly Schaafsma has written that these artists were "highly concerned with decorative effects and the elements of design, which in most instances take on a geometric quality."

Societies like the Fremont, which come from a strong hunter-gatherer tradition, tended to place responsibility for religious activities and healing rituals in the hands of specialized practitioners or shamans. These individuals had techniques to induce out-of-body experiences to make contact with supernatural powers. Rock art such as you see at the Dry Fork Canyon site often is interpreted in terms of shamanic rites. At this site, however, you can also find images that show evidence of warfare: shields and figures holding what appear to be severed heads.

You will notice that each petroglyph panel has been marked by the letter "P" and a number. This scientific desecration can be credited to Albert B. Reagan, who surveyed and reported on this area in the 1930s. Such practices are no longer acceptable and are unlawful on public land.

If you spend a morning seeing the Dry Fork Canyon petroglyphs, you will have time to visit the quarry, Swelter Shelter, and Cub Creek petroglyphs at Dinosaur National Monument (p. 181) in the afternoon. The Harpers Corner Trail in the monument offers a two-mile round-trip hike to a scenic point overlooking Echo Park and the confluence of the Yampa and Green rivers. Vernal offers many travel services. A series of camping areas can be found further up Dry Fork Canyon.

Suggested reading: *The Rock Art of Utah,* by Polly Schaafsma, University of Utah Press, Salt Lake City, Utah, 1994.

*Petroglyph panel of bighorn sheep and hunters. Courtesy Polly Schaafsma.*

## Nine Mile Canyon

*Nine Mile Canyon is 21 miles north of Wellington, Utah, which is 7 miles south of Price. From U.S. 6 in Wellington, take the Nine Mile Canyon turnoff (Soldier Creek Road). After 12 miles of pavement, the road turns to gravel. Information: (435) 636-3600.*

Despite its name, Nine Mile Canyon is forty miles long. Legend tells that it was named for an early pioneer family named Miles, which consisted of the two parents and their seven children. The truth, however, more likely lies in confusion surrounding early survey maps.

Nine Mile Canyon, whose creek drains into the Green River to the east, is noted for its extensive collection of Fremont rock art sites. There are ruins here as well. Although the gravel road usually is well maintained, it is a considerable excursion from the main highway to this remote canyon, especially if you come from Mynton to the north. Once arrived, more driving and walking is required to see the petroglyphs. Thus, to have a full day of exploring sites in the canyon, start early and bring a picnic.

You can explore Nine Mile Canyon on your own using a guidebook or brochure—a couple of printed ones are on the market, or check the Internet for one you can download. Or you can hire a personal guide or join an organized tour group. Either way, you will see plenty of petroglyphs.

Many sites require only a short walk from the road. Published guides give you a starting point to set your odometer at zero and then follow mileages to recommended stopping points along the road. The densest panels are along the lowest cliffs and near the mouths of side canyons.

Nine Mile Canyon is in what archaeologists refer to as the Northern San Rafael zone of the Fremont culture. You will note that the style of the rock art here differs markedly from the Classic Vernal Style in Dry Fork Canyon (p. 186). The anthropomorphs, for example, are much diminished in size and lack the presence and emotional impact of the imposing figures near Vernal. While they are solidly pecked out, they do not exhibit the fine workmanship or elaborate decoration of the northern style. Many panels are crowded with pictures, among which human figures account for a much smaller percentage than further north. You will see an abundance of quadrupeds as well as birds, snakes, insects, hand and paw prints, and abstract patterns. The latter include wavy and meandering lines, patterns of dots, and concentric circles and spirals.

The bighorn sheep is a common motif in Nine Mile Canyon, as is the hunter. One well-known panel in Cottonwood Canyon, a tributary of Nine Mile Canyon, includes nearly thirty sheep, which are headed toward a group of hunters with bows and arrows. Among the sheep is a trapezoidal anthropomorphic figure with horns. It has been suggested that the scene portrays a shaman using his powers to direct a herd of sheep toward waiting hunters. Historically, Indian hunters are known to have used a similar method. An individual with special or magical powers would cover himself with an antelope skin complete with head and horns, drop to all fours, and slowly integrate himself into a herd. Then he would gradually lead the grazing antelope to hunters hiding nearby.

Nine Mile Canyon also contains the remains of dwellings of the Fremont, who inhabited the area between A.D. 1000 and 1250. Often, they are small masonry structures tucked in cliffs or built high on a ridge with a commanding view. Unlike Anasazi builders, the Fremont laid up their stone walls without the use of mortar, and the walls of most houses have long since tumbled down or been pushed over by cattle. Given the scale of the landscape—a wide valley whose cliffs rise to a thousand feet above the floor—the remains of the old Fremont dwellings are difficult to see. Using your guide and a pair of binoculars, however, you should be able to spot several ruins.

There are a number of ranches in Nine Mile Canyon, which are private property. The owners ask that visitors respect their privacy and follow posted instructions regarding trespassing and access. As the canyon has become an increasingly popular attraction, maintaining harmonious relations with its residents is important. When you hike to these remote sites, please be sure that everyone in your party is aware of appropriate archaeological etiquette and does not inadvertently damage the petroglyphs.

The nearest travel services are in Wellington and Price. Reflections on the Ancients (435/637-7336) is a tour company in Wellington specializing in Nine Mile Canyon tours. If you are traveling north, you will find more Fremont rock art in Dry Fork Canyon and Dinosaur National Monument (p. 181). If you are headed south, refer to chapters on Moab (p. 178), Sego Canyon (p. 13), and Buckhorn Wash (p. 11).

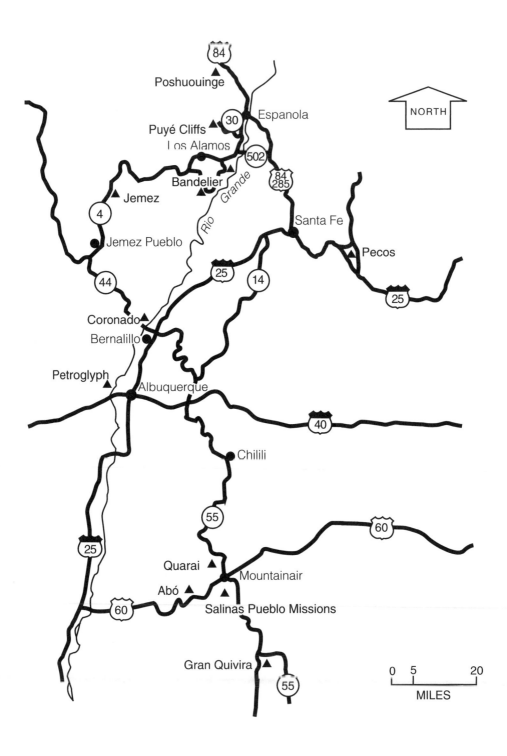

Rio Grande Area

# Pueblos and Missions
# of New Mexico

I n sixteenth-century New Mexico, two cultural threads in
Southwestern history—Native American and European—became
inextricably entwined.

When Anasazi culture in the Four Corners region collapsed in the
late 1200s, places like Mesa Verde, Grand Gulch, and Canyon de Chelly
were left vacant. Many Four Corners Anasazi—refugees, if you will—
migrated to new areas, including the Rio Grande region. As the newcomers moved in and displaced some of the local residents, new villages
were founded. Poshuouinge (p. 203), for example, appeared in the
lower Chama River valley; Tyuonyi Pueblo was constructed in what is
now Bandelier National Monument (p. 196); and the pueblo of Kuaua
(p. 208) was founded north of present-day Albuquerque. By the 1500s,
farming communities of various sizes, whose members spoke half a
dozen different tongues, were thriving along the Rio Grande corridor
from the foothills of the Rockies to the Gulf of Mexico.

The second thread was European. In 1540, a Spanish army replete
with mounted knights in glittering armor approached the Zuni pueblo
of Hawikuh in central-western New Mexico. On a summer afternoon,
the two cultures came face to face, conflict erupted, and the Pueblo
world was catapulted into a new era. The effects of the contact between
Spaniard and Indian were immediate, and even after four and a half centuries, they remain a subject of controversy.

Diseases from Europe, such as influenza and smallpox, devastated the
health of indigenous Americans. Untold numbers died. In the
Southwest, a new religion from Europe was introduced to—indeed,
often forced upon—native people who held very different spiritual
beliefs. Europeans and Indians had widely differing value systems, too.

*Pictograph of Spanish riders, Canyon de Chelly.*

For one—to oversimplify—the natural world presented a challenge to be overcome and exploited for gain; to the other, nature was a supernatural force to be lived with in harmony.

In the more tangible world, horses were introduced, as well as cattle, sheep, and goats. Their presence affected the economy, the environment, travel, and methods of warfare. Then there were metals and minerals, rifles and cannons, new crops and technologies. Each new element forced changes on traditional ways of living.

In the arid environments of the Southwest, people have always gravitated to water. As you would expect, the most desirable lands are along streams and in river valleys. It logically came about, therefore, that many Spanish settlements grew up near Indian pueblos. In some instances, Spanish settlers moved right into Pueblo villages, welcome or not, to obtain shelter and protection. Franciscan missionaries always took up residence among their Indian flock and had the natives build churches and mission buildings—a huge expenditure of time and energy.

*Doorway of the mission church at Pecos.*

Over the years and centuries, the two disparate cultures intermingled, sometimes in a spirit of cooperation, sometimes in an atmosphere of coercion and conflict.

Steeped as New Mexico's history is in complex cultural and human relationships, it holds much fascination. The differences between Spanish and Indian perspectives, combined with the stresses inherent in trying to survive in a harsh environment, often evoked extreme responses in human behavior. The most dramatic manifestation of this was the Pueblo Revolt of 1680, sometimes called the First American Revolution. During this upheaval, Franciscan priests were killed, churches burned, colonists driven into exile, and independence regained for twelve years by scores of Indian communities.

To learn about all these events, you can turn to a wealth of historical literature. But there is another way: Get in your car and go to some of the places where, as it were, history happened. Enter an ancient cave dwelling, place your hand on the walls of a crumbling mission church, or examine mythic figures pecked on a cliff face, and the past comes alive.

## Bandelier National Monument

*Bandelier National Monument is near Los Alamos, New Mexico, 46 miles west of Santa Fe. From Santa Fe, take U.S. 285 north. At Pojoaque, follow N.M. 502 toward Los Alamos, then turn off on N.M. 4 to the monument. (One mile from the 502/4 intersection, you will pass the parking area for Tsankawi, a unit of Bandelier.) Information: (505) 672-3861. Entrance fee.*

Adolph F. Bandelier (1840–1914), for whom this monument is named, is a legendary figure in the annals of Southwestern anthropology. At the age of forty, this Swiss-born Illinois businessman, who had a passion for historical research, boarded a train for Santa Fe—1880 was the year the railroad reached New Mexico's capital city—to begin an intense study of New Mexico's Indian cultures. He initially survived on a small allowance from the Archaeological Institute of America. Bandelier traveled great distances on foot, crossing mountains and deserts, and persevering through winter storms, fatigue, and sickness. His pioneering efforts as an observer of indigenous customs, recorder of story and myth, and surveyor of prehistoric ruins established him as the first anthropological scholar of the American Southwest.

Adolph Bandelier's first visit to Frijoles Canyon, which is in the heart of Bandelier National Monument, was on October 23, 1880. He had a guide from Cochiti Pueblo, where he had been staying. That evening he scribbled in his journal, "the grandest thing I ever saw. A magnificent growth of pines, encina [oak], alamos [poplars], and towering cliffs, of pumice or volcanic tuff, exceedingly friable." He went on to describe the impressive ruins he was shown in the canyon. "There are some of one, two, and three stories. In most cases the plaster is still in the rooms. Some are walled in; others are mere holes in the rocks." Bandelier's southwestern journals give a daily account of his journeys and discoveries over the next several years.

*Adolph F. Bandelier, anthropologist and historian. Courtesy Museum of New Mexico.*

Frijoles Canyon and the surrounding area on the Pajarito Plateau eventually were set aside by the federal government, thanks in large part to the conservation and political efforts of Edgar Lee Hewett, an archaeologist who was a friend and admirer of Bandelier. The park is as rich in pre-Columbian resources as it is in scenic beauty. The oldest site in the park has been dated to 2010 B.C., and other Archaic-period campsites have been found along the Rio Grande that were in use between 670

*Tyuonyi Ruins, Bandelier National Monument.*

and 590 B.C. From the river to the mountains, hunter-gatherers had access to an abundance of natural resources: animal, mineral, and vegetal.

Although Pueblo Indians had been living and farming in the Rio Grande Valley since around A.D. 600, they did not colonize the Pajarito Plateau until the late 1100s. Immigrants settling in the valley then may have pressured local inhabitants to move up on the plateau. Initially, the Pajaritans lived in extended-family dwellings or small pueblos, probably relocating every few years in search of fresh land to till.

In the 1300s, however, as more immigrants from the Four Corners region arrived in the Rio Grande Valley, the Pajarito population grew dramatically. At the same time, the majority of the population came together to live in a dozen large villages. Some well-known examples are Tshirege, Otowi, and Puyé (p. 201), which lie outside the park boundaries, and Tyuonyi, a circular pueblo on the floor of Frijoles Canyon near the visitor center. The large, unexcavated pueblo of Tsankawi is in a separate unit of the monument. Typically, these centers, some of which had over six hundred rooms, consisted of multistoried roomblocks built around a spacious central plaza with a kiva. The trend toward large population centers suggests the development of a new, more centralized, sociopolitical order such as the Spanish observed when they arrived in New Mexico in 1540.

Because of the plateau's geology, most large pueblos are associated with what archaeologists refer to as cavates. These are naturally formed concavities in the cliffs that the Indians expanded to live in or use for storage or kivas. With stone hammers and chisels, they hollowed these rooms out of the soft volcanic tuff. In front of the cave dwellings, they sometimes built masonry houses. Holes in the cliff where they anchored roof beams are still clearly visible.

As most families lived in large villages, they sometimes had to travel considerable distances to their scattered fields. For convenience, therefore, they built small summer houses to use while tending their crops. If you hike to Tsankawi, you will see grooves that are deeply worn or excavated into the tuff. These are ancient trails, which, in addition to marking travel routes, may also have served a ceremonial function.

While the residents of Frijoles Canyon farmed intensively, they also collected wild plants and hunted rabbits and mule deer. Hunting and gathering would have been especially important in years of crop failure. They may have fished the Rio Grande, too, although little evidence of this activity shows up in the archaeological record.

One wonders why people eventually left Tyuonyi, Long House, and the many other pueblos of the Pajarito Plateau. This same question arises in connection with many other areas throughout the Southwest that were once intensely inhabited. While speculations revolve around drought, depleted resources, exhausted soils, and warfare, answers are hard to find. The cave dwellings and pueblos of Frijoles Canyon and the Plateau in general are believed to have been vacant by the mid-1500s. The descendants of the Pajarito people presently live along the Rio Grande in the Tewa-speaking pueblos of San Ildefonso and Santa Clara and the Keresan pueblos of Cochiti and Santo Domingo.

Bandelier National Monument offers a variety of possible experiences, depending on your time and endurance. At a minimum, spend two hours exploring the main Frijoles Canyon sites. Additional options include walking up to Ceremonial Cave, hiking to the Rio Grande, taking the mile-and-a-half Tsankawi trail loop, or backpacking to the more remote sites of San Miguel, Yapashi, Painted Cave, and the Stone Lions shrine.

Facilities in the monument include a campground on the mesa, an attractive picnic area along Frijoles Creek, and a visitor center with a well-stocked bookstore. Nearby attractions include Puyé Cliff Dwellings, San Ildefonso Pueblo, and driving up into the mountains to view the Valle Grande, the world's largest caldera. Tourist services are available in Los Alamos, Española, and Santa Fe.

Suggested reading: *The Delight Makers,* by Adolph F. Bandelier, Harcourt Brace Jovanovich, New York, 1971.

# Puyé Cliffs

*The ruins at Puyé Cliffs are located on the Santa Clara Indian Reservation south of Española, New Mexico. From Española, take New Mexico 30 south for 5 miles, turn west, and proceed another 7 miles to the ruins park. Information: (505) 753-7326. Fee.*

Puyé (poo-yay) is one of several very large late-prehistoric pueblos on the Pajarito Plateau. Its story closely parallels that of sites in nearby Bandelier National Monument (p. 196). This park, which is managed by Santa Clara Pueblo, is a popular attraction for tourists in Santa Fe and northern New Mexico for its archaeological resources and scenic beauty.

Like Bandelier, Puyé is situated on the eastern flank of the Jemez volcanic field. Just over a million years ago, the Jemez Mountains experienced a series of cataclysmic eruptions, or pyroclastic flows. Hundreds of cubic miles of volcanic ash and cinders exploded into the air, the heavier material pouring down the mountainside to form the broad, sloping Pajarito Plateau with its deep deposits of pumiceous rock or tuff. Since then, erosion has cut a series of narrow, sheltered canyons, such as Frijoles at Bandelier, which attracted inhabitants. They benefitted from a varied environment with an abundance of resources and more rainfall than was received by the lower Rio Grande Valley.

The northern sector of the plateau, where Puyé is located, saw its first permanent Puebloan settlements in the 1200s, when population throughout the region was on the increase. In the 1300s, the Pajaritan farmers began to aggregate into towns, sometimes two-storied and shaped like a horseshoe with the opening facing east. Still later, the horseshoe was closed to form an interior plaza with a kiva, surrounded on all sides by terraced apartments. In the 1400s, the trend toward larger communities reached a peak when the northern Pajaritan population gravitated to five towns: Tsankawi (p. 200), Tshirege, Navawi, Otowi, and Puyé. Puyé, one of the largest, had more than a thousand rooms.

The pueblo sits on top of a mesa and is built of blocks of tuff that the Indians shaped with stone tools. Its multistoried quadrangle of apartments was stepped back to form a protected inner court in which the residents carried out their daily chores, played, raised turkeys, and performed religious ceremonies. The limited access to the plaza offered a degree of defense against potential attackers.

Below the mesa, the Puyé residents built more apartments with back rooms excavated into the friable rock. These cliff dwellings, which extend for at least a mile, housed many more people. Over the centuries since Puyé was abandoned, the cliffside buildings have fallen down, but the cavates remain and may be explored by visitors. One group of rooms along the cliff has been restored.

*View from inside a cave dwelling, Bandelier National Monument.*

*Mesatop ruins at Puyé.*

Like the residents of Frijoles Canyon at Bandelier, the Puyé Indians grew corn, squash, and beans below their dwellings, making use of the creek that flows out of Santa Clara Canyon to irrigate their garden plots. They hunted deer and elk in the hills and rabbits and rodents in the piñon-juniper woodlands. A variety of plants served as sources of food, medicine, and dyes.

The archaeologist, Edgar Lee Hewett, who founded the Museum of New Mexico and other anthropological institutions in the Southwest, surveyed the northern Pajarito Plateau in the 1890s and excavated a small part of Puyé in 1907. He started an archaeological field school and one of his first students, Sylvanus G. Morley, excavated Puyé's South House in 1909. These were the first systematic archaeological excavations to take place in the northern Rio Grande region, but unfortunately, only general descriptive notes were kept, and no detailed report was ever published. In that early era of archaeological research in America, emphasis was placed more on opening up sites and collecting artifacts than on trying to reconstruct cultural developments and collective human behavior.

Puyé and other towns on the Pajarito Plateau were vacated in the 1500s, shortly before the arrival of Spaniards in New Mexico. Puyé's inhabitants moved down closer to the Rio Grande, probably to found Santa Clara Pueblo. The Santa Clarans manage the site and regard Puyé as an ancestral home.

When you go to Puyé, you can park at the bottom of the mesa, walk up a trail to the cave dwellings, and continue to the top, where the main pueblo ruins are located. Alternatively, you can drive to the mesa top and start walking from there. Puyé's walls have been rebuilt to about waist high to give visitors a visual, if somewhat inauthentic, sense of the pueblo's layout. One kiva has been restored, and sometimes visitors are allowed to climb down the ladder to see the interior. Little archaeological or historical interpretation is offered in the park.

At this park, you will find drinking water, toilets, picnic tables, and camping in nearby Santa Clara Canyon. Travel services are available in Española.

Suggested reading: *Pajarito Plateau Archaeological Survey and Excavations,* by Charlie R. Steen, the Los Alamos Scientific Laboratory of the University of California, Los Alamos, New Mexico, 1977.

# Poshuouinge

*Poshuouinge is located along U.S. 84, 2.5 miles south of Abiquiu, New Mexico. A trail leads from a parking area off the highway to a hill overlooking the site and the Chama River. Information: (505) 753-7331.*

Although the Chama River Valley is one of the richest archaeological regions in New Mexico, its prehistory is little known to the public. At least a dozen major pueblos and hundreds of smaller sites have been recorded by archaeologists, but only a few have undergone extensive study. Like a library, these resources hold much potential for future research.

Poshuouinge (poe-shoo-wingay), which lies in the lower Chama valley, is ancestral to the Tewa Indians, who presently live in a series of pueblos near Española. The closest are San Juan and Santa Clara.

Thirteenth-century migrations of Anasazi–Pueblo people from the Four Corners region had a major impact on the existing population of the Rio Grande region. Many locals left their homes to establish new communities up the Chama River Valley. Poshuouinge (*poshu* means "muddy river" and *ouinge* is the Tewa term for village), which sits on an terrace overlooking the Chama, is a good example. Other sites such as Tsama, Sapawe, Tse Ping, and Posi, are much less accessible.

Poshuouinge was founded around A.D. 1400 and within two generations had become a thriving community. Its residents found many advantages to living in this valley: plenty of water from the Chama and its tributary streams, arable land along the river and on its terraces, and excellent foraging and hunting in the nearby uplands. The valley also was a travel and trade corridor between the southern Rockies and the Rio Grande.

When feasible, Pueblo farmers diverted runoff water to their fields or carried water in pots from a nearby stream or river. In the Chama region, archaeologists also have found the remains of thousands of so-called grid gardens, which were delineated by river cobbles and covered by gravel. This stone mulch helped to conserve moisture, moderate soil temperatures, and keep down weeds. It was a clever local adaptation to farming in high, arid conditions.

Poshuouinge, like scores of other villages in the area, survived until 1500 or so, when its inhabitants began moving to the valley of the Rio Grande. It is doubtful that any of the Chama communities were still inhabited when Coronado's expedition explored this region in 1540–1541.

Adolph F. Bandelier, the famous explorer-anthropologist for whom the nearby national monument is named, visited Poshuouinge in 1885, but not until 1919 were formal excavations conducted at the site. The archaeologist, J. A. Jeancon, dug 137 rooms and produced a report that consists mainly of an inventory of artifacts that he unearthed. It lists many stone tools, such as polishing stones for floors, andirons, mortars, and arrow shaft polishers. Bone implements included awls, tanning tools, breastplates, turkey calls, flutes, spatulas, and knives.

Jeancon and his crew uncovered ceramic pipes, dishes and vessels, gaming pieces (Indian gambling did not begin with casinos), spindle whorls, and pot lids. Among ceremonial items found were fetishes, ceramic cloud blowers, and lightning stones, the last being small, smooth, white quartzite pebbles that produce a faint flickering light resembling distant lightning when rubbed briskly together in the dark.

Poshuouinge had about seven hundred ground-floor rooms surrounding two large plazas, in one of which the remains of a large kiva is visible. The pueblo was mostly one- and two-storied, possibly with one three-storied section. Its walls were built of adobe mud mixed with river cobbles. After the site was abandoned and rains eroded the mud mortar, the walls melted to low mounds capped by scatters of stones.

A well-marked trail leads from the parking area up the terrace. It skirts along the edge of the ruins and on to a bench and ramada overlooking the site. If you continue to the top, you will discover an even better view of the valley, a circle of stones once used as a shrine, and a pictorial reconstruction of how the pueblo appeared centuries ago. You should allow yourself forty-five minutes to an hour or so to do the full hike. Please stay on the trail and do not collect any artifacts.

Food, gas, and accommodations are available in Abiquiu and Española. In nearby Abiquiu, the home of Georgia O'Keeffe may be visited by appointment and Puyé Cliffs (p. 201) are only a short drive away.

Suggested reading: *Valley of Shining Stone: The Story of Abiquiu,* by Lesley Poling-Kempes, University of Arizona Press, Tucson, Arizona, 1997.

# Petroglyph National Monument

*Petroglyph National Monument is located along Albuquerque's West Mesa in New Mexico's middle Rio Grande Valley. From its intersection with Interstate 25 in Albuquerque, drive 6 miles west on Interstate 40 and take the Unser Boulevard exit (#154). Follow Unser north for 3 miles to the monument's entrance on the left. Information: (505) 899-0205.*

Petroglyph National Monument, the only unit of the National Park Service devoted solely to preserving rock art, was established in 1990. The petroglyphs, numbering more than fifteen thousand are concentrated in three primary areas within this seven-thousand-acre park. To see them, you can explore a variety of trails requiring from fifteen minutes to a couple of hours to walk.

The petroglyphs appear on boulders of basalt along the seventeen-mile escarpment of Albuquerque's West Mesa. This geologic formation is the eastern edge of a lava flow that poured from a fissure three miles to the west some 110,000 years ago: a recent event in earth history. The geologic context of the rock art is a fascinating dimension of this monument and is part of its interpretive program.

The oldest rock art you may see here was made by hunter-gatherers during the Archaic period (p. 5) two thousand or more years ago. A few of these ancient markings, often consisting of circles, squiggly lines, and curvilinear abstract designs, can be found in the vicinity of a series of extinct volcanoes on the west side of the monument.

While examples of early Pueblo rock art also are present in this extensive collection, the majority of the petroglyphs are in the Rio Grande Style, which dates from about A.D. 1300 to 1700. The early fourteenth century, when many Anasazi were emigrating from the Four Corners region, was a dynamic period in the Rio Grande Valley. Population was

*Rock art at Petroglyph National Monument.*

on the rise, new ideologies were appearing, and Pueblo society was undergoing rapid change. These developments are reflected in the iconography of the rock art. Petroglyphs of bear shamans and badgers suggest the presence of medicine societies; faces, masks, and ceremonial figures relate to the newly arrived kachina cult; star beings and mountain lions reflect war symbolism.

At the end of the seventeenth century, Spanish colonists, including Franciscan missionaries, had an impact on Native American society in the Rio Grande Valley. Spanish authorities adamantly repressed Pueblo religious life and especially cracked down on the kachina rituals. After the Pueblo Revolt of 1680, little rock art seems to have been produced by the Pueblos. Some European markings, however, occasionally appear. Spanish sheepherders, for example, etched Christian crosses next to the Indian glyphs to counter what they believed were the evil effects of pagan symbols.

Archaeologists have recorded numerous Pueblo IV village sites along the Rio Grande between Albuquerque and Bernalillo, a region Vasquez de Coronado called the Province of Tiguex. It is all but certain that the inhabitants of these pueblos were responsible for making the petroglyphs. Today, their descendants from the Tiwa-speaking pueblos of Isleta and Sandia advise the monument how to manage and curate the petroglyphs. As one Pueblo leader expressed it, "To us these petroglyphs are not the remnants of some long lost civilization that has been dead for many years...they are part of our living culture."

Ever since a local group of rock art enthusiasts first began the process of protecting West Mesa's petroglyphs in the 1970s, conflicts have arisen between preservationist and development interests. Population growth has spurred development on Albuquerque's west side, with the result that residences, roads, and vehicles have encroached upon the escarpment, degrading open lands and threatening historic and sacred cultural resources. In recent years, one hotly debated issue has been whether or not to build a highway through the park. Another concerns how much to develop its trail system. More information on this subject can be obtained at the monument or from Friends of the Albuquerque Petroglyphs, 2920 Carlisle N.E., Albuquerque, NM 87110, (505) 889-3779, www.igc.org/fotap/.

Petroglyph National Monument has three units with trails to petroglyphs: Boca Negra Canyon, Rinconada Canyon, and Piedras Marcadas Canyon. Rangers at the visitor center will help you decide which walks will best suit your available time and ability. While in the Albuquerque area, you may also wish to visit the Maxwell Museum of Anthropology at the University of New Mexico and Salinas Pueblo Missions National Monument (p. 214) in the vicinity of Mountainair.

Suggested reading: *Signs of Life: Rock Art of the Upper Rio Grande,* by Dennis Slifer, Ancient City Press, Santa Fe, New Mexico, 1998.

# Coronado State Monument

*Coronado State Monument is located along New Mexico 44, 1 mile west of Bernalillo and 16 miles north of Albuquerque. Information: (505) 867-5351. Entrance fee.*

The ruins of Kuaua Pueblo at Coronado State Monument lie along the west bank of the Rio Grande with a view of the Sandia Mountains to the east. Its low mud walls, eroding under each passing rainstorm, are a lingering reminder of the life and culture that flourished here before the arrival of Europeans.

Kuaua was settled in the fourteenth century, when Puebloan groups from the west were migrating to the Rio Grande Valley. The pueblo consisted of multistoried adobe apartment blocks surrounding three spacious plazas in which the residents built kivas, or underground ceremonial chambers. Like many Pueblo villages, Kuaua seems to have been designed with defense in mind: Its high, doorless exterior walls meant that anyone coming to the village had to enter by way of narrow passageways, that could be barricaded.

The residents of this pueblo, it is believed, spoke the southern dialect of Tiwa, the language of present-day Isleta and Sandia pueblos. (The Indians of Taos and Picuris pueblos speak a northern Tiwa dialect.) Their main resource was the life-giving Rio Grande. The Indians irrigated gardens of corn, beans, and squash along its margins and hunted a variety of animals and migrating waterfowl that were attracted by the water and lush vegetation. The riverine environment also produced many useful wild plants and medicinal herbs. The Sandia Mountains across the Rio Grande offered good hunting, too, and other natural resources.

Kuaua is a proto-historic site: it was occupied before and after the coming of Europeans. A detachment of Vasquez de Coronado's army found its way to the Rio Grande Valley in the summer of 1540. Later that year, Coronado brought his full expeditionary force—three hundred soldiers, a thousand Indian allies and servants, and fifteen hundred horses and mules—here to spend the winter. Although they certainly visited Kuaua, they appropriated another nearby pueblo, Alcanfor, for their quarters, displacing its inhabitants.

The Spaniards counted a dozen pueblos along the river between Isleta Pueblo and Kuaua and called this the Province of Tiguex. During the winter of 1540–1541, they made themselves extremely unwelcome among the Indians. Conflicts arose over the Spaniards' appropriation of supplies and the alleged molestation of a Pueblo woman. In retaliation, the Indians drove off some of the Spanish horses. When open warfare broke out, Coronado's soldiers overwhelmed two Tiwa pueblos, destroying one entirely and killing many of its inhabitants. The events of that winter set the stage for an adversarial relationship between

*Eroding remains of Kuaua Pueblo.*

Pueblo and Spaniard that eventually led to the Pueblo Revolt of 1680.

Coronado's chronicler, Pedro de Castaneda, recorded his observations of Indians doing house construction.

> They all work together to build the villages, the women being engaged in making the mixture and the walls, while the men bring the wood and put it in place. They have no lime, but they make a mixture of ashes, coals, and dirt which is almost as good as mortar, for when the house is to have four stories, they do not make the walls more than half a yard thick.

The Pueblos originally puddled the adobe mud on the walls, allowing each course to stiffen before laying another on top. Today, you will notice that the pueblo's walls are made of adobe bricks: These are the result of restorations in the 1940s.

The highlight of archaeological investigations at Kuaua, which took place in the 1930s, was the discovery of a kiva containing seventeen layers of colorfully painted murals. After the murals were carefully removed—some are presently on view in the visitor center—the kiva was restored and its murals redone as an interpretive exhibit.

*Restored kiva and murals at Coronado State Monument.*

Kuaua was abandoned around 1700 and never reoccupied. Although archaeological evidence does not shed light on why the Indians left, it is known that the Pueblo Revolt and its aftermath caused much turmoil and dislocation in the Pueblo world. Another possible factor was the steep drop in Pueblo population as a consequence of epidemic diseases such as smallpox and influenza.

Coronado State Monument has picnic sites overlooking the Rio Grande. In addition to the display of original murals, the visitor center has historical exhibits. An interpretive trail leads through the ruins. In a single day, you could easily visit this site, Jemez State Monument (p. 220), and Petroglyph National Monument (p. 205).

Suggested reading: *Coronado: Knight of Pueblo and Plains,* by Herbert E. Bolton, University of New Mexico Press, Albuquerque, New Mexico, 1991.

## Pecos National Historical Park

*Pecos National Historical Park is located off Interstate 25, approximately 25 miles east of Santa Fe, New Mexico. From Santa Fe, take the Glorieta-Pecos exit and proceed 8 miles through Pecos village to the monument. Southbound travelers on I-25 should take the Rowe exit and continue 3 miles to the ruins. Information: (505) 757-6031. Entrance fee.*

In 1927, Alfred Vincent Kidder invited his colleagues to come to

Pecos Ruins to view his diggings and discuss common archaeological problems and issues. When they arrived, they had an opportunity to see firsthand Kidder's thoroughly scientific approach to doing archaeology. Up to this time, the objective of most fieldwork was to collect artifacts for museums. Kidder's work at Pecos, begun in 1915, is now recognized as a landmark in the development of North American archaeology. In addition, the 1927 gathering gave birth to the annual Pecos Conference, which still continues.

Pecos Ruins are situated on a rocky knoll in the middle of a wide fertile valley. Nearby, the Pecos River flows out of the high mountains to the north and continues its long journey through New Mexico to join the Rio Grande in Texas. High mesas border the valley to the south and to the west lies Glorieta Pass, a gateway to the Rio Grande Valley and the site of a Civil War battle. From the ruins, the valley descends gradually eastward, to open on the southern Great Plains.

Geography, beyond providing the people of Pecos with a beautiful and varied environment, played a part in the life and history of the pueblo. Close by were fertile farmlands, reliable springs, and fuel wood; the high country was rich in game and timber; and materials for making tools, weapons, pottery, and basketry were also close at hand. But what gave Pecos a special advantage was its strategic location between the agricultural Pueblo communities of the northern Rio Grande and the nomadic hunting tribes of the plains. Trade became a lucrative factor in the pueblo's economy. The Pecos Indians profited from their role as middlemen, but not without cost, for they frequently found themselves the target of raids by Comanches, Apaches, and Caddoans.

Sometime after A.D. 800, Puebloan settlers in the Rio Grande Valley moved into the upper Pecos valley to form small, scattered pithouse hamlets. Their population grew slowly for several centuries; then, after A.D.1200, it suddenly increased, probably as a result of immigration. Pecos Pueblo, founded around A.D. 1300, eventually grew to nearly seven hundred rooms built in multilevel community houses around a central quadrangle. Its commanding position and fortress-like design allowed its inhabitants to defend themselves effectively against outside attack.

The Pecos Indians, who spoke the Towa language, eventually reached a population estimated at fifteen hundred or more. Less than fifty years after Columbus landed in the New World, they were visited by the conquistador Vasquez de Coronado, who was searching for wealth beyond Mexico's northern frontier. Mistrustful of the Spaniards, the Pecos Indians enticed Coronado to follow his dream onto the vast windswept plains to the east, a good place to lose one's way.

After Coronado's visit, Pecos was spared further contact with Spaniards until 1590, when Castaño de Sosa stormed and occupied their pueblo with a small but well-armed force. In his account, Castaño wrote that Pecos had four-story high apartment blocks, which its inhab-

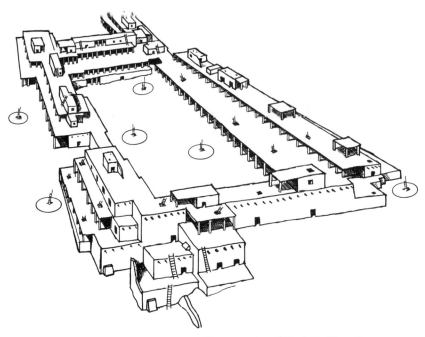

*Reconstruction of North Pueblo at Pecos.*

itants reached by ladders. He noted that the men wore cotton blankets under a buffalo robe, and the women were dressed "with a blanket drawn in a knot at the shoulder and a sash the width of a palm at the waist." Over this garb they wore colorful blankets or turkey feather robes.

In 1618, using Indian labor, Franciscan monks established a mission just east of Pecos Pueblo, which later included a massive adobe church and convento (living quarters for the padres) complete with carpenter shop, weaving rooms, tannery, stable, and school. They introduced wheat, orchards, metal tools, animal husbandry, and Christianity, but suppressed the Indians' own religious practices. One of Kidder's findings was a cache of smashed clay figurines and a stone "idol" that had been broken and repaired.

The Indians destroyed the Pecos mission in their 1680 rebellion against Spanish rule, but it was rebuilt in the early eighteenth century. The 1700s were hard on the natives. Epidemics of fever, measles, smallpox, and other pestilences decimated the population, and they were repeatedly attacked by Comanches and Apaches. By the latter part of the century, the pueblo's once proud five-hundred-warrior force had been so reduced that the Indians depended on the Spaniards for defense. By 1838, less than twenty souls remained here, and these last occupants trekked eighty miles northwest to live at Jemez Pueblo. In 1999, the descendants of the Pecos Indians at Jemez Pueblo received back a large collection of their ancestors' skeletons and grave goods, which had been stored in anthropological institutions in the East. It is the largest return

*Ruins of the massive adobe church at Pecos National Historic Park.*

of artifacts from a single site under the Native American Graves Protection and Repatriation Act.

You will be most impressed by the monumental ruins of Pecos's eighteenth-century church, which overlies an earlier and even larger church. After seeing the monument's fine museum, pick up a trail guide and take the scenic walk to the old pueblo, the church and convento, and two restored kivas. On summer weekends, native artisans demonstrate how to make traditional crafts.

In recent years, Pecos National Historical Park acquired most of the adjacent Forked Lightning Ranch, which belonged to Greer Garson and Buddy Fogelson. The Park offers tours of the historic ranch buildings.

Pecos village, located two miles from the monument, has places to eat, a general store, and a gas station. Camping, fishing, and picnic sites can be found a few miles up the Pecos River canyon. From Santa Fe, a trip to Pecos makes a pleasant and interesting half-day excursion.

Suggested reading: *Kiva, Cross, and Crown: The Pecos Indians and New Mexico, 1540–1840,* by John L. Kessell, University of New Mexico Press, Albuquerque, New Mexico, 1987.

# Salinas Pueblo Missions National Monument

*The headquarters of Salinas Pueblo Missions National Monument are at the corner of Broadway and Ripley streets in Mountainair, New Mexico. The monument has three nearby units—Gran Quivira, Quarai, and Abó—where you can explore the remains of Indian pueblos and Spanish missions. Information: (505) 847-2585.*

Named for a string of salt flats and shallow ephemeral lakes, the historic Spanish province of Las Salinas lies in New Mexico's Estancia Valley. These "lakes" actually are the remnants of a large brackish body of water that filled the basin in the last Ice Age. Paleo-Indian hunters (p. 1) stalked mammoths and other Pleistocene animals along the water's margins eleven thousand years ago.

After A.D. 600 or so, the Salinas region began to see its first permanent human settlements in the form of pithouse hamlets. Their occupants, who made unpainted reddish-brown pottery, were probably of Mogollon stock. By A.D. 900, the Salinas Indians were constructing above-ground masonry pueblos resembling those used by the Anasazi-Pueblo inhabitants of the Four Corners region. The Salinas pueblos grew into full-fledged apartment complexes in the 1200s, and when Spanish troops explored the region in 1598, the pueblo of Las Humanas (later known as Gran Quivira) rivaled Pecos in size and strength.

The Salinas missions were established by Franciscan priests soon after Don Juan de Oñate founded Spain's first colony in New Mexico in 1598. From this time until the mid-1670s, Spanish missionaries, supported by soldiers, were active in the Salinas Province. The remains of the churches they built then with Indian labor are a testimony to their fervent efforts to Christianize the Native American community.

The pueblos and missions of Las Salinas are a poignant reminder of a turbulent period in New Mexico's past, when Native Americans first came in contact with Europeans. While the present chapter can only briefly touch on these events, you may find that a visit to the sites will be a catalyst to read more about them. An excellent starting point is *Salinas Pueblo Missions,* by Dan Murphy (Southwest Parks and Monuments Association, Tucson, Arizona, 1993). You should set aside a full day to visit all three units of the monument. The town of Mountainair has several cafes, a motel, shops, and other travel services, and the cities of Socorro, Belen, and Albuquerque are not far away.

*The ruins of Las Humanas Pueblo (foreground) and
San Buenaventura Mission at Gran Quivira.*

## Gran Quivira

*Gran Quivira is located 26 miles south of Mountainair on New Mexico 55.*

Exposed to the winds and scarce in water, the pueblo of Gran Quivira seems an unlikely spot for any settlement. But it had a large population of Tompiro-speaking Indians who held a lively trade with the buffalo-hunting tribes of the southern Plains to the east. It was the presence of one of these tribes, the Humanas, that gave this town its original Spanish name.

Archaeological research has been conducted at Gran Quivira several times, beginning in the 1920s. One curious bit of evidence points to an influx of people here from the Zuni area in the 1540s. The newcomers cremated their dead and made Zuni-style pottery. It is thought that after Vasquez de Coronado attacked the Zunis in 1540, a group of these Indians left their home country to start a new life here.

Coronado's army never visited the Salinas pueblos, but in 1598, Oñate led a force of four hundred mounted troops here. What an impression they must have made upon the Indians, who had never seen horses, let alone knights in armor! The conquistadores routinely conducted a brief ritual at each pueblo in which an Indian leader expressed submission to the king of Spain. One wonders, however, if the significance of the rite often was lost in translation.

There are two church sites at Gran Quivira. The first church, named for San Ysidro, the patron saint of farmers, was built in the 1620s. Twenty years later, construction began on a full mission complex, which included a larger church, sacristy, baptistry, dining hall, patio, living quarters for the padres, workshops, stables, and corral. Due to a series of delays, this mission was never completed, and for most of its existence, Gran Quivira was attended by a priest who lived in far-off Abó.

Gran Quivira, even more than the other Salinas missions, was located far from Santa Fe. While distance from the Spanish capitol had its benefits to the Indians, there were disadvantages, too, for the Salinas towns came under repeated attack by Plains tribes in the mid-1600s. They had already been weakened by the Spanish system of tribute, known as the encomienda, and by the effects of European diseases, including smallpox and influenza. Then drought struck. In 1668, when 450 Gran Quivirans died of starvation, the pueblo's demise was near. Between 1672 and 1675, the pueblo's survivors packed up their belongings and took refuge among communities along the Rio Grande.

With its extensive excavated Indian and Spanish ruins, Gran Quivira is an impressive place to visit. There is a new visitor center and museum here, a picnic area, and an interpretive trail through the site.

Suggested reading: *Excavations in a 17th-Century Humano Pueblo, Gran Quivira*, by Gordon Vivian, U.S. National Park Service, Archaeological Research Series 8, Washington, D.C. 1964.

## Quarai

*Quarai is located in Punta de Agua, 8 miles north of Mountainair on New Mexico 55.*

The church at Quarai, Nuestra Señora de la Purisima Concepcion de Cuarac, is nestled in a cottonwood grove in a small valley just outside the hamlet of Punta de Agua. Its massive sandstone walls still dominate the pastoral environs. Adjacent to the mission ruins and predating them by several centuries are the mounds of a Tiwa Indian pueblo, Acolocu,

*La Purisima Concepcion church at Quarai.*

which once stood two to three stories high. The Tiwa language is spoken today at the pueblos of Isleta and Sandia, near Albuquerque.

In 1601, warriors from Quarai joined Abó in defense against a punitive attack by Spanish forces. After a prolonged battle, the Indians were overwhelmed and, according to Spanish reports, nine hundred of them were killed and two hundred more taken captive. A similar battle had been fought between Spanish and Indian forces at Acoma Pueblo shortly before this one, with the same results. These two events helped cement Spanish authority over the Pueblo Indians in New Mexico, at least until the great rebellion of 1680.

Quarai became the seat of New Mexico's Holy Inquisition, in which individuals were investigated and punished for such offenses as gossip, heresy, blasphemy, witchcraft, use of love potions, and disrespect to the clergy. In one of Quarai's cases, a trader, Bernardo Gruber, was accused of superstition. The unfortunate man languished in jail for more than two years without ever going to trial. His possessions were appropriated, his stock died, and his own health began to fail. Finally, with the help of an Indian ally, he broke out of his cell and fled south only to perish from thirst in the desert. That desert is still called the Jornada del Muerto, "journey of the dead man."

Another name associated with Quarai is that of the priest, Geronimo de la Llana who was well liked by his flock during the decade he ran the mission. After he died in 1659, his remains were repeatedly disinterred and reburied before finding a final resting place in the crypt of St. Francis Cathedral in Santa Fe.

Quarai's history is marked by stress and conflict. Built-in ethnic and cultural tensions were exacerbated by the behavior of the community's *encomendero* (tribute collector), on the one hand, and resident priests, on the other. It was a situation in which the local Indians constantly lost ground. For reasons similar to those at Gran Quivira, the mission at Quarai failed. By 1678, two years before the Pueblo Revolt, this community was but a memory.

Quarai has a small museum relating to its Spanish-Colonial history. An interpretive trail leads past Acolocu to the church. You can picnic here and camp in nearby Manzano Mountains State Park.

Suggested reading: "Quarai: A Turbulent History," by John P. Wilson, in *Salinas: Archaeology, History, Prehistory,* edited by David Grant Noble, Ancient City Press, Santa Fe, New Mexico, 1993.

## Abó

*To reach Abó, drive 9 miles east of Mountainair on U.S. 60, then 1 mile north. The turn from Route 60 is well marked.*

The spring at Abó was the lifeblood of this community. It nourished aboriginal gardens, then quenched the thirst of Spanish conquistadores, later fed the boilers of railroad steam engines, and today serves the needs of a small Hispanic community.

Not many yards north of the spring lie the unexcavated mounds of a large Tompiro pueblo and, adjacent to it, the ruins of the mission of San Gregorio de Abó. Like Gran Quivira and Quarai, this church was the product of the fervent missionizing enterprise organized by the Franciscans in the seventeenth century. Strategically situated between the salt lagoons and the Rio Grande Valley, and in an area of good piñon nut harvests, Abó was a reasonably well-off community. It was reportedly from the sale of piñon nuts, in fact, that the mission was able to afford the purchase of a church organ in 1661.

The salt beds of Salinas were an important commodity, attracting Indians from a wide region. They were also treated as neutral ground

*The Abó mission complex.*

where conflicts or hostilities were put aside. Local folk, of course, were best positioned to profit from the trade in salt. When excavating Gran Quivira, archaeologists found a large chunk of salt in a storage room, apparently awaiting transport to a distant market. The Spanish, too, needed salt both for domestic use and to process silver ore in their mines in Parral. They exported large quantities of Salinas salt to Parral, in Mexico, along with Apache slaves to work the silver mines.

The mission of Abó only functioned for about fifty years. During this time, relations between Indian and Spaniard fluctuated from warfare to cooperation and cordiality. This pattern was true at numerous pueblos of the period in New Mexico. Indeed, when Spanish forces returned to New Mexico in 1692, some former Pueblo adversaries collaborated with them as they reconquered their lost territory.

When Adolph F. Bandelier visited Abó in the 1880s, local residents told him they remembered seeing the Indian ruins standing three stories high forty years earlier. Today, an interpretive trail winds among the mounds and on to another, older site across the wash. The mission ruins were excavated in the 1930s by Joseph H. Toulouse, Jr. While he did not find remnants of the old church organ, he did locate a kiva in the west patio that was built at about the same time that the church was in use. Since the Franciscans strongly disapproved of native pagan rites, its existence here is something of a puzzle. Toulouse also uncovered the remains of turkey pens within the mission walls and recovered Old World watermelon and mission grape seeds. Grape growing here predates that of the California missions by more than a century.

At Abó, as at Quarai, Gran Quivira, and other New Mexico missions, you will be impressed by the ramifications of contact between two very disparate cultures. The story of these seventeenth-century pueblos and missions had both heroic and tragic dimensions. In the end, both cultures survived and learned to accommodate each other.

Suggested reading: *The Mission of San Gregorio de Abó,* by Joseph H. Toulouse, Jr., Monograph No. 13, School of American Research, Santa Fe, New Mexico, 1949.

# Jemez State Monument

*Jemez State Monument is along New Mexico 4 in Jemez Springs, New Mexico. It is 55 miles north of Albuquerque and 30 miles southwest of Los Alamos. Information: (505) 829-3530. Entrance fee.*

The ancestors of the Jemez Indians are believed to have moved to the southern Jemez Mountains around five hundred or six hundred years ago. Both oral traditions and archaeological traces point to their having lived in the upper San Juan River country to the north prior to moving here. Farther back still, it is likely that they were part of the Mesa Verdean branch of the Anasazi.

Beginning with Coronado in 1541, several early Spanish expeditions explored the Jemez country, describing the Jemez as a strong nation residing in seven pueblos. These villages, which extended along the Jemez River or were perched on mesa tops, held a population estimated at seven or eight thousand people. One of the valley towns, Giusewa (pronounced Jee-say-wah), was located near some hot springs. The Spaniards' early forays into the land of the Jemez apparently took place without mishap or conflict and had little impact on the Indians' way of life.

In 1598, when Juan de Oñate led a large colonizing expedition to New Mexico, serious Catholic missionary work was begun among the region's many Indian tribes. In that same year, a padre was assigned to the Jemez Indians and probably moved into Giusewa Pueblo. Confronted by many difficulties, his efforts and those of his successors faltered repeatedly.

It was not easy for missionaries to reach the scattered pueblos and then they found that Indians, who had their own highly developed religion, did not welcome Christianity. To alleviate their task and to be able to exercise better control over the native people, the Spanish civil authorities tried to concentrate groups of small pueblos into a single large village. While this system served Spanish interests, it was highly inconvenient to the Jemez and disruptive to their society and economy. Concentrated living also fostered the spread of contagious diseases.

During the seventeenth century, relations between the Jemez Indians and their Spanish rulers deteriorated. One failed Indian insurgency, supported by the Navajos, resulted in twenty-nine Indians being executed. In 1675, a Jemez religious leader accused of witchcraft was hanged in Santa Fe's plaza along with other Pueblo religious leaders. When the Pueblo Revolt broke out five years later, the Pueblos destroyed churches and killed priests and settlers throughout New Mexico. The survivors of the rebellion fled into exile in El Paso. The missionary at San José de los Jemez, built in 1621 next to Giusewa Pueblo, was among the martyred Franciscans.

The Jemez Indians strongly resisted Spanish attempts to reconquer New Mexico between 1692 and 1696. At this time, most of the population, joined by other Pueblo freedom fighters, retreated to defensive sites on the mesa tops. In 1694, Diego de Vargas, the new governor of New Mexico, successfully attacked the pueblo of Astialakwa, which sat on a narrow, steep-sided mesa overlooking the Jemez River. Eighty-four Indians died in the battle and 361 were taken prisoner. Others became refugees among the Navajos, who lived in the Dinetah region (p. 223) to the west. At this time, Vargas also recovered the body of the priest slain fourteen years before, finding his corpse still pierced by arrows.

When peaceful conditions finally settled over the Jemez Valley, the Indians took up residence in Walatowa, located a few miles south of Jemez Springs. Known now as Jemez Pueblo, their descendants still live there today. Meanwhile, Giusewa and San José church fell into ruins. Today, Giusewa consists of a series of brush-covered mounds. The walls of the church, however, which were built up to eight feet thick, still stand as a formidable monument to New Mexico's Spanish-Colonial past. Its interior measures 111 feet in length by 34 feet across. Twelve pedestals, which probably supported statues of the disciples, stand along the nave. A set of stairs lead up to the altar behind which a forty-two-foot octagonal turret suggests a defensive purpose.

Archaeologists conducted excavations at Giusewa and San José mission in 1910, 1920–1921, and again between 1935 and 1937. Unlike the research done by Alfred V. Kidder at Pecos Ruins (p. 210), these investigations were far from exemplary. Artifacts and skeletons were removed, but scientific findings never were published and even field notes were lost. Perhaps the most exciting discovery in the church ruins was a series of frescoes on the nave walls. The fresco technique, involving the application of paint to wet plaster, was rare in New Mexico ecclesiastical art. Fleur-de-lis and other floral patterns and realistic Indian motifs in green, blue, yellow, red, black, and white were found. Also of interest were remnants of windows made of selenite, a translucent form of gypsum.

*San José de los Jemez Church, Jemez State Monument.*

Jemez State Monument, administered by the Museum of New Mexico, has a visitor center and small museum. An interpretive trail leads across the mounds of Giusewa, past an excavated kiva, through the church and convent, and around the mission courtyard. As the site is nestled in a narrow valley, you will find this to be a pleasant and interesting walk through New Mexico and Indian history.

Jemez Springs has restaurants and accommodations. A visit to Jemez Pueblo might be of interest, especially on its Feast Day of November 12, when dances are performed in the plaza. If you drive north on Route 4, you will pass Bandelier National Monument (p. 196), a fascinating archaeological park in a beautiful canyon.

Suggested reading: *Jemez,* by Michael Elliot, Museum of New Mexico Press, Santa Fe, New Mexico, 1993.

# Pueblitos of Dinetah

*The Pueblitos of Dinetah are scattered throughout the Largo and Gobernador river drainages northeast of Farmington, New Mexico. To obtain detailed directions and information on road conditions, call the Farmington Field Office of the Bureau of Land Management at (505) 599-8900.*

Dinetah, which surrounds the Largo and Gobernador rivers in northwestern New Mexico, is where the Navajo Indians first lived after migrating to the Southwest. They still regard Dinetah as their original homeland and a place of historic and mythical significance.

The Navajos are an Athapaskan people whose ancestors long ago migrated south from northern Canada, probably reaching the Southwest in the 1400s. Other Athapaskans, or Apaches, roamed the plains and mountain regions farther to the east and south. The Navajos and Apaches supported the Pueblo Indians in their 1680 rebellion against Spanish rule. Conflicts between the Indians and Spaniards reignited twelve years later, when the latter returned to regain their lost territory.

In the early 1700's many Pueblos went west to the canyon-cut Dinetah area, where they lived among the Navajos. For several generations thereafter, the two disparate groups, who often had enjoyed less than friendly relations, lived side by side in the remote and inaccessible Dinetah. They made a life together, shared customs, and often intermarried.

During the early 1700s, a new threat presented itself to all settlements in northern New Mexico: raiding parties of Ute Indians, who by now had horses. In defense, the inhabitants of Dinetah fortified themselves in small stone structures, called pueblitos. Fort-like in design, they often were perched on promontories or large boulders or on the rims of canyons to better view approaching enemies. Many were built of uncut sandstone blocks and appear to have been put up in haste. In some respects, they resemble the towers of Hovenweep (p. 67), which were built by ancestral Pueblo Indians centuries before, possibly under similar circumstances.

Near most of the pueblitos are traces of Navajo hogans and roasting pits. The characteristic "forked stick" hogan of the period was made by first leaning together three cedar poles as a tripod structure, then placing more poles against these to form a conical framework that was covered by bark and earth. Some of these old hogan remains can still be seen today and, in some cases, the support poles remain upright.

Since the Dinetah had limited areas suitable for farming and grazing stock, it could not support a growing resident population. By 1754, most of the Navajos had moved to new territories south and west. The Pueblos either went with them or returned to the Rio Grande region.

*A pueblito in Dinetah.*

The period of coexistence of Navajos and Pueblos in Dinetah saw a blending of the two formerly distinct cultural traditions, as well as a genetic mixing through intermarriage. The Navajos adopted and modified some aspects of Pueblo religion and ceremonialism, and several new Navajo clans were formed at this time.

Dinetah contains ancient habitation and rock art sites as well as landscape features that figure prominently in Navajo mythology. Some traditional Navajos know the location of these sites and visit them. Considering the importance of this region in Navajo culture, it is unfortunate that it was found also to contain huge oil and gas reserves. Since the 1950s, Dinetah, which is administered by the Bureau of Land Management, has undergone intensive development. Drilling sites have proliferated, connected by a network of roads to accommodate heavy truck traffic.

In recent years, the Bureau of Land Management has opened eight pueblitos and one rock art site to the public as part of its national "Adventures in the Past" program. If you are interested in visiting these sites, you should contact the BLM field office in Farmington for directions. Be prepared to drive forty to a hundred miles on unpaved roads. A high-clearance vehicle is recommended. Truck traffic in this area can be intimidating, and in wet weather the dusty roads turn to mud. The BLM can suggest local agencies or companies that offer guided tours of the Dinetah.

While exploring the Dinetah may not be for everyone, the sites are rewarding for the insight they offer to Navajo and Pueblo history. You will find travel services in Bloomfield and Farmington. Other nearby archaeological sites include Salmon Ruins (p. 132), Aztec Ruins National Monument (p. 128), and Chaco Canyon (p. 113).

Suggested reading: "Navajo Prehistory and History to 1850," by David M. Brugge, in *Handbook of North American Indians*, vol. 10, edited by Alfonso Ortiz, Smithsonian Institution, Washington, D.C., 1983.

# Afterword
## The Future of the Past in the Southwest

The ancient sites described between these covers represent only a small fraction of the archaeological resources that exist throughout the Southwest. Indeed, many of the nonarchitectural remains that are scattered about the Southwest's landscape usually are passed by without notice by the nonprofessional observer. Still, every potsherd, projectile point, and subtle man-made alteration of the landscape contributes to the story of our collective past.

As we enter the twenty-first century, the future of the Southwest's archaeological heritage appears increasingly uncertain. To be sure, the ruins of Mesa Verde and other national parks are safe. But on other public lands, where mining, logging, and other forms of development are encouraged, the value of archaeological sites frequently is balanced against the exploitation of natural and recreational resources. And what about private land, where our national patrimony is most at risk?

Archaeological sites, like forests and farmlands, are threatened by the many consequences of population growth: expanding cities and suburbs, multiplying roads and utility lines, and increased sightseeing, hiking, and off-road vehicular driving. Another significant problem is looting. The lucrative international market for antiquities tempts more and more people to pillage ruins. Sunday pothunters with probe sticks have been augmented by bulldozers and backhoes that can quickly and destructively churn through an entire village site.

The question is, what can be done? The greatest help in preserving our archaeological resources from looting and vandalism will come from the vast pool of people who appreciate and value the Southwest's cultural and natural environments. These include hunters, fishermen, hik-

*Cave Dwelling at Bandelier National Monument.*

ers, backpackers, bird watchers, horseback riders, photographers, naturalists, ruins buffs, and many others. To all who want to safeguard ruins, here are some suggestions.

1. Be sure that when you visit archaeological sites, you and your family or companions do not climb on walls, disturb ruins, touch rock art, or collect artifacts.
2. If you see signs of recent or current pothunting or vandalism, report it right away to the land owner or manager or local law enforcement authority. If you observe any of the activities proscribed in the Archaeological Resources Protection Act of 1979 (see following section), take appropriate action. Photographs, license numbers, and descriptive information all are useful in apprehending offenders.
3. Should you become aware of a proposed development or land-disturbing activity that might damage an archaeological site, become an advocate and work with local political bodies to find an acceptable solution to the problem.
4. Support and/or participate in educational activities that communicate the value of our cultural heritage including archaeological resources. This can be done through museums, cultural and civic organizations, or school systems, and can be as simple as telling a scout troop about your visit to Mesa Verde.
5. Support The Archaeological Conservancy, a national membership organization that preserves archaeological sites so that they may be studied and enjoyed by future generations. The Conservancy's address is 5301 Central Avenue N.E., Suite 1218, Albuquerque, NM 87108-1517; (505) 266-1540; e-mail: archcons@nm.net.

America's archaeological treasures are part of our national heritage, something in which we should all take pride. They are sacred to Native Americans, an inspiration to writers and artists, and an irreplaceable source of information to historians, social scientists, tourists, and school children. Let's do all we can to help keep these valuable resources intact. It is the author's hope this book will make its own contribution by generating wider public appreciation of southwestern antiquity, and that it will have a positive effect on preserving our archaeological heritage for the future.

# Archaeological Resources
## Protection Act of 1979

PUBLIC LAW 96-95, 31 OCTOBER 1979

To protect archaeological resources on public lands and Indian lands, and for other purposes.

## FINDINGS AND PURPOSE

Sec. 2(a) The Congress finds that—

(1) archaeological resources on public lands and Indian lands are an accessible and irreplaceable part of the Nation's heritage;

(2) these resources are increasingly endangered because of their commercial attractiveness;

(3) existing Federal laws do not provide adequate protection to prevent the loss and destruction of these archaeological resources and sites resulting from uncontrolled excavations and pillage; and

(4) there is a wealth of archaeological information which has been legally obtained by private individuals for noncommercial purposes and which could voluntarily be made available to professional archaeologists and institutions.

(b) The purpose of this Act is to secure, for the present and future benefit of the American people, the protection of archaeological resources and sites which are on public lands and Indian lands, and to foster increased cooperation and exchange of information between governmental authorities, the professional archaeological community, and private individuals having collections of archaeological resources and data which were obtained before the date of the enactment of this Act.

## PROHIBITED ACTS AND CRIMINAL PENALTIES

Sec. 6(a) No person may excavate, remove, damage, or otherwise alter or deface any archaeological resource located on public lands or Indian lands unless such activity is pursuant to a permit issued under section 4, a permit referred to in section 4(h)(2), or the exemption contained in section 4(g)(l).

(b) No person may sell, purchase, exchange, transport, receive, or offer to sell, purchase, or exchange any archaeological resource if such resource was excavated or removed from public lands or Indian lands in violation of—

(1) the prohibition contained in subsection (a), or

(2) any provision, rule, regulation, ordinance, or permit in effect under any other provision of Federal law.

(c) No person may sell, purchase, exchange, transport, receive, or offer to sell, purchase, or exchange, in interstate of foreign commerce, any archaeological resource excavated, removed, sold, purchased, exchanged, transported, or received in violation of any provision, rule, regulation ordinance, or permit in effect under State and local law.

(d) Any person who knowingly violates, or counsels, procures, solicits, or employs any other person to violate, any prohibition contained in subsection (a), (b), or (c) of this section shall, upon conviction, be fined not more than $10,000 or imprisoned not more than one year, or both; Provided, however, That if the commercial or archaeological value of the archaeological resources involved and the cost of restoration and repair of such resources exceeds the sum of $5,000, such person shall be fined not more than $20,000 or imprisoned not more than two years, or both. In the case of a second or subsequent such violation upon conviction such person shall be fined not more than $100,000, or imprisoned not more than five years, or both.

REWARDS: FORFEITURE

Sec. 8(a) Upon the certification of the Federal land manager concerned, the Secretary of the Treasury is directed to pay from penalties and fines collected under sections 6 and 7 an amount equal to one-half of such penalty or fine, but not to exceed $500, to any person who furnishes information which leads to the finding of a civil violation, or the conviction of criminal violation, with respect to which such penalty or fine was paid. If several persons provided such information, such amount shall be divided among such persons. No officer or employee of the United States or of any State or local government who furnishes information or renders service in the performance of his official duties shall be eligible for payment under this subsection.

# Index

Note: italicized page numbers indicate pictures.

**D**avid Grant Noble is a writer and photographer living in Santa Fe, New Mexico. Other books he has written include *Pueblos, Villages, Forts, and Trails: A Guide to New Mexico's Past* and *101 Questions About Ancient Indians of the Southwest*. During his years at Santa Fe's School of American Research, he edited a series of well-known books on archaeological and historical areas of the Southwest, among them *New Light on Chaco Canyon* and *The Hohokam: Ancient People of the Desert*. His photographs have been exhibited in galleries and museums around the country.